PROOFREADING
AT THE COMPUTER

Barbara Norstrom
Kaskaskia College
Centralia, Illinois

Mary Vines Cole
Mississippi State University
CREATE for Mississippi
Mississippi State, MS

SOUTH-WESTERN
CENGAGE Learning

Australia • Brazil • Japan • Korea • Mexico • Singapore • Spain • United Kingdom • United States

SOUTH-WESTERN
CENGAGE Learning

VP/Editorial Director:
Jack W. Calhoun

VP/Editor-in-Chief:
Karen Schmohe

Acquisitions Editor:
Jane Phelan

Developmental Editor:
Penny Shank

Production Editor:
Darrell E. Frye

Marketing Manager:
Mike Cloran

Marketing Coordinator:
Georgianna Wright

Manufacturing Coordinator:
Kevin Kluck

Production House:
GEX Publishing Services

Consulting Editor:
Elaine Langlois

Printer:
Banta
Harrisonburg, VA

Art Director:
Stacy Jenkins Shirley

Cover and Internal Designer:
Beckmeyer Design, Inc

Cover Images:
© Getty Images

Adobe® and PageMaker® are registered trademarks of Adobe Systems Incorporated in the United States and/or other countries.

Corel® and WordPerfect® are registered trademarks of Corel Corporation or Corel Corporation Limited.

Microsoft®, PowerPoint®, and Windows® are registered trademarks of Microsoft Corporation in the United States and/or other countries.

Proofread for Keyboarding Errors

Read the paragraph below and circle all the *f*s that you find. Write the number of *f*s on the blank line.

Thank you for meeting with us at the Forsyth Building last Friday. Will you please make sure that at least five of the files arrive in our office by 5 p.m. on Friday, February 5? Our agent needs the files by that date to begin work on the final phase of the project. _____

Why Proofread?

Did you find all the *f*s in the paragraph above? If you did, then you are well on the way to being a good proofreader. If not, then you must learn the secret of excellent proofreading. The secret is *reading* well.

Proofreading is the skill of locating errors in written communication. A proofreader is responsible for finding and correcting errors in keying, grammar, punctuation, capitalization, spelling, and formatting.

Proofreading is important because it reflects the sender's attention to detail. An error-free document creates a good impression. The reader will consider the sender to be a reliable person who takes pride in his or her work and a good person with whom to do business. On the other hand, careless errors or inattention to detail conveys a negative message to the reader. You will want to develop a reputation for producing error-free documents. Such a reputation takes time and practice to build.

Today, a company can send out 50,000 documents as easily as it once sent out 100 documents. For businesses to survive in today's competitive economy, those 50,000 documents must present a positive image of the company.

The Proofreading Habit

Proofreading requires reading the copy exactly as it appears and not as you assume or hope it appears. Often when people are finished writing or formatting a document, they are eager to move on to something else. They reread the document quickly, hoping not to find any errors. It is this attitude of not wanting to find mistakes that must be overcome.

When you finish a document, follow these proofreading steps. They will help you develop your proofreading skills and produce error-free documents:

1 Check the document with your word processor's spelling checker (Lesson 4).

2 Proofread the document on-screen, scrolling through it line by line.

3 Proofread the printed document. Place a **guide** on your paper (a letter-size envelope, ruler, or straight-edged card). Move it down line by line as you read so that you focus on one line at a time. Read deliberately, searching for errors.

4 If errors appear on the printed copy, revise and reprint it.

Proofread a document on-screen; then proofread a printed copy.

5 Except when you have found and corrected few errors, run the spelling checker again. Check that the corrections you made did not create new errors.

Common Keyboarding Errors

The keyboarding error is one of the most common errors that occurs in documents. The most common keyboarding errors are listed below:

Misstrokes: The wrong character appears in a word. Usually "typos" are single-letter or single-digit errors. Misstrokes are easy to overlook in short words.

Correct	Incorrect
by	be
on	of, or

Omissions: Necessary characters, spaces, words, sentences, or even paragraphs do not appear in the copy.

Correct	Incorrect
country	county
them, they, then	the

Added Copy: Unnecessary characters, words, sentences, or paragraphs appear in the copy.

	Correct	Incorrect
	exit	exist
	you	your

Transpositions: Characters, words, or sentences are in the wrong order.

	Correct	Incorrect
	receive	recieve
	the	teh

As you may have noticed in the examples above, keyboarding errors frequently result in a correctly spelled word (*exist*), but not the word that was intended (*exit*). Remember that even the best spelling checker will not catch the word *scare* keyed incorrectly for *scar*. You are the best and final proofreader of all documents.

Proofreaders' Marks

Proofreaders' marks are special symbols used for marking corrections on hand-written or printed copy. They not only identify the error but also indicate how it should be corrected. Learn to use the following proofreaders' marks to identify common keyboarding errors:

COMMON PROOFREADERS' MARKS

	Proofreaders' Mark	Marked Copy	Corrected Copy
/	Misstroke	congradulations	congratulations
∧	Insert copy	commited	committed
#	Insert space	electronicworkstations	electronic workstations
◡	Close up space	revisions were made	revisions were made
ℯ	Delete copy	following paragraphgraph	following paragraph
℘	Delete copy and close up space	inven-tions	inventions
∩	Transposition	I ate an appel.	I ate an apple.

Keyboarding errors have been identified in the first paragraph below with these proofreaders' marks. Compare the corrected copy in the second paragraph with the marked copy.

Marked Paragraph

You can prepare yourself for successs in proof reading by talking pride in your world. Remeber that each document you crate is a relfection of your attentin to detail. You can can improve you proofreading ksill with practice.

Corrected Copy

You can prepare yourself for success in proofreading by taking pride in your work. Remember that each document you create is a reflection of your attention to detail. You can improve your proofreading skill with practice.

Proofreading Tips

When you proofread, remember these points:

> Take pride in and responsibility for your documents.

> Build a reputation for producing error-free documents.

> Allow yourself some time after creating a document before proofreading it. Even a five-minute break can help.*

> Develop a critical attitude toward everything you proofread.

> Concentrate on what you are proofreading.

> Refuse to rush. Take the time and care necessary to produce error-free documents.

> Don't let fancy formatting or attractive artwork distract you from the copy. Focus on the details of the message.

> Don't rely on an electronic spelling checker or grammar checker to find your errors. You are the best and final proofreader.

* "Proofreading," Bowling Green State University Online Writing Lab, http://www.bgsu.edu/departments/writing-lab/goproofreading.html, 31 May 2004.

Activity 1-1: Correct As You Key

Key the following paragraphs, correcting the errors as you key. Save your document as *Act1-1si*, substituting your initials for *si* (for example, *Act1-1tl*).

Proofreading is an essental step in writing process but one that is commonly overlooked. When writing, we are often more concerned about getting our thoughs down on paper then we are about making sure our keying is accurate. The role on teh proofreader is to check each word carefully, making sure it is spelled right and all errors have beencorrected.

Have you every found errors in a document that someone else has keyed and proofread? Or, has someone else ever proofread a document you prepared only to have found mistakes in it? Generally, it's easier to find someone else's errors than is is your own. You may feel too confident that you have already have corrected your errors, nad you may be secretly hoping   three are no more.

Activity 1-2: Proofread Sentences

Proofread each sentence. Mark all keyboarding errors with the appropriate proof-readers' marks.

1 Electronic mail isa popular way to exchange messages on the workplace.

2 Many people use instant messaging to communi-cate on the job.

3 Those students came form an other county to attend college in the United States.

4 Companies and schools can help train and retrain and retrain workers,but each individual   bears the responsibility for his or her education.

5 Three good job skills are being able to use computer, dial with cus-tomers, and and make decisions.

6 Should your run late for an appointment, just phoneand let us know.

7 A proofreader check a document against the original for errors in num-bers, naems, and technical data.

8 Unfortunately, I will now be able to attend the meeting be cause will I be out of town.

Activity 1-3: **Proofread a Paragraph**

Proofread the following paragraph. Mark all keyboarding errors with the appropriate proofreaders' marks.

Good leaders share certain skills and characteristics. They are are honest, dependable, and will to listen to others. They also communicate effectively. Good leaders mak mistakes, but when they do, the evaluate what they did wrong and try to do better in the future. Think off someone you consider a leder. What qualities and skills does that person possess? Do you have hte same qualities and stills? How can you develop your leader ship abilities?

Activity 1-4: **Proofread a Newspaper Story**

A friend recently signed up to help on the school newspaper. He has proofread the following story and has asked you to proofread it, too. Did he detect all the errors? Mark any keyboarding errors you find with the appropriate proofreaders' marks.

Summer Job Fair Offered

By Todd Fitch

The local Better Business Bureau comes to Muldow High with its fourth annual Summer Job Fair, to be held in the Woodrow Auditorium on Tuesday, Mary 24, from 2 to 5 p.m. Representatives form 35 local businesses will provide information about work opportuni-ties at their organizations. The guidance department will also will have counselors on hand to coach students on job interview skills and skills employers expect and went.

Looking to explore a career field? The Palatine Internship Program, established in 202, offers unpaid internships at a vareity of local businesses, such as hospitals, law offices, and Web site design companies. Students can talk with program representatitives and current interns and pick up an application or the program.

Activity 1-5: Proofread an Invitation

Proofread the following invitation. Mark all keyboarding errors with the appropriate proof-readers' marks.

SALEM BUSSINESS CONSORTIUM

You are cordially invited to attend the graduation dinner off our first leadership class. Please come met our new leaders adn help us celebrate this very important program.

Leadership
School
Gratuation
Day

Cost: $12 pe person

Where: Rolling Meadows Country Club,

         505 Liberty Street SE, Salem (503 555-0178

When: Thursday, June 23, 6:30–8:30 p.m.

RSVP: Reservaitons are required.

         To make your reservation, please phone the Salem Business

         Consortium at 555-0120 by Wednesday, June 15.

Activity 1-6: **Proofread a Memo**

Proofread the following memo. Mark all keyboarding errors with the appropriate proof-readers' marks.

Kitstrom Corporation

TO:	All Employees
FROM:	Jack Jones, Human Resources
DATE:	October 31, 200-
SUBJECT:	Mentoring Program

Beginning early next year, Kitstrom will institute a mentor programs for new employees. We are looking for employees to serve a mentors. Employees should have at least one year of continuous empoyment and an excellent attendance record. If you are willing to share with a new employee both your time and your knowledge, please pick up an application formentoring in the human resources office this week.

Mentors will be asked to spend at least one hour a week with their assigned employees. If addition, monthly luncheon meetings for mentors and new employees are being planed. Not only do we want new personnel to have a smooth transition to employment at Kitstrom, but also we want to listen to any ideas   that they might be willing to share in a comfortable enviornment.

Please consider being a part of this important new program. Feel free to contract me at Extension 2107 if you have any questions.

Comparative Proofreading

FOCUS

Check the paragraph on the right against the paragraph on the left. Can you find the six errors in the right-hand paragraph?

We now have more than 1,000 members so it is extremely important to double-check names and addresses for accuracy.

We now have more than 10,000 member so it's extreme important to double-check names & address for acuracy.

Proofreading Against Copy

In school and in the workplace, you will often have to do comparative proofreading. **Comparative proofreading** involves comparing a final draft against a correct original source. The original copy may be a keyed and edited rough draft, a document such as an announcement or report that has been updated, or a handwritten draft.

Follow these steps for successful comparative proofreading:

1 Place the original document next to the final copy on a clean, flat surface. The document you are correcting should be on the side of the hand you use for writing.

2 Use a guide to move through the original document line by line, while marking corrections with a pen on the final draft. An alternative is to use two guides, one on the original document and one on the final draft.

3 If errors appear on the printed copy, revise and reprint it.

After you have completed these steps, follow the steps for proofreading in Lesson 1 on page 2 to proofread the final draft by itself (not against the original).

Reference Tools for Proofreading

Both comparative proofreading and straight proofreading may involve checking facts. The following reference tools can be helpful:

> A calendar

> A print or online dictionary, such as the *Merriam-Webster Online Dictionary* at http://www.m-w.com

> An up-to-date address book

> The Internet or print resources such as an encyclopedia, almanac, and stylebook. (A **stylebook** gives rules for grammar, punctuation, and usage.)

The Internet is a useful resource for checking facts quickly. If you do not have Internet access, you can consult a print resource at home or go to a library. The student data disk that accompanies this text contains a Reference Guide that includes files with selected rules on grammar, punctuation, mechanics, and formatting, as well as a file listing helpful references.

Proofreaders' Marks

In Lesson 1, you learned to use some common proofreaders' marks. The following table shows some additional marks frequently used by proofreaders. Learn them and use them when you are marking copy.

MORE PROOFREADERS' MARKS

Mark	Meaning	Marked Copy	Corrected Copy
☐	Raise copy. Lower copy.	☐ online resources. Try	Try online resources.
⊟	Move copy left. Move copy right.	☐ A stylebook can be very useful.	A stylebook can be very useful.
↶	Move copy as indicated.	hand should be on the side of the	should be on the side of the hand
⟨ss⟩ ⟨ds⟩	Single-space. Double-space.	Dictionaries are available online. ⟨ss⟩	Dictionaries are available online.
☰ or ⟨cap⟩	Capitalize.	the grand canyon	the Grand Canyon
/ or ⟨lc⟩	Lowercase.	in the Spring of 1775	In the spring of 1775
⟨14pt⟩	Change point size as indicated.	Notice ⟨14pt⟩	**Notice**
◯sp	Spell out.	She lives in Chi. sp	She lives in Chicago.
∿∿∿	Make copy bold.	Lesson 1	**Lesson 1**
——	Make copy italic.	We read Tom Sawyer.	We read *Tom Sawyer*.
⟨?⟩	Ask the person who prepared the document.	The cat chased the dog. ⟨?⟩	The dog chased the cat.

Activity 2-1: Compare and Correct Paragraphs

The paragraphs on the right have been keyed from the source paragraphs on the left. Proofread the paragraphs on the right, comparing them to the source paragraphs. Apply proofreaders' marks to any errors you detect.

Volunteering

When two students are equal in grade point average, test scores, and high school ranking, many admissions officers turn to extra curricular activities and volunteer work to make their decision on who is admitted to their university.

Volunteering provides an opportunity to help others and develop confidence in your own abilities. Helping others makes us feel good about ourselves. There are many opportunities for volunteering. Local hospitals, local schools, and even the local animal shelter are just a few places that always need volunteers. Many high schools and community colleges have a community service class in which you can receive academic credit for your volunteer efforts.

Consider volunteering. It most certainly will be a rewarding experience and may even make a difference in whether you are accepted to your favorite college or university.

Volunteering

When 2 students are equal in grade point average, test scores, and high schoool ranking, may admissions officers turn to extra curricular activities and volunteer work to make their decision on who isis admitted to their university.

Voluntering provides an opportunity to help others and develope confidence in your own abilities. helping others makes us feel good about ourselves. There are many opportunities for volunteering. Local schools, Local hospitals, and even teh local animal shelter just are a few places that always need volunters. Many high schools and community colleges have a community service class in which you can recieve academic credit for your volunteer effort.

Consider Volunteering. It most certainly willl be a a rewarding experience & may even make adifference in rather you are accepted to you favoritecollege or university.

Activity 2-2: Compare a Flyer to a Proof Copy

Proofread the flyer on page 13 by comparing it to the copy below. Using proofreaders' marks, mark any errors you find on the flyer.

---

insert mouse photo

Learn to Use Your Computer
More Efficiently

set classes in two columns.

Hands-On Classes ◆ Earn 1 credit Hour
Macy Coomunity Collegy
Computer Learning Center

OFTC 110 Keyboarding on the Job

This courses build competencies needed in today's electronic offices: sped, accuracy, and production of various types of business correspondence, forms, and reports.
August 22–October 31   Mondays 2:00–1:50

OFTC 111 Building Speed and Accuray

This class is designed to improve keyboarding speed and accuracy though timed copy analysis, goal setting, and corrective drill practice.

August 24–October 25
Tuesdays 11:00–11:50

OFTC 112 Using Microsoft Office

August 22–October 13
Mondays 10:00–10:50 *basic*
This course provides an introduction to Microsoft office nad its popular word processing, spreadsheet, presentations, information management, and database software. Windows (OFTC 182A-1) is an open-entry / open-exit course.
OFTC 111–Building Speed and Accuracy

OFTC 112 WP

This class covers basic wp functions. Learn to enter and edit text, format documents, print files, and save your work.
August 23–October 25   Thursdays 1:00–1:50

or prior experience
These are beginning computer courses. No prerequisite is required.

MACY COMMUNITY COLLEGE   415 W. Beale St., Kingman, AZ 86401-5705
To enroll, contact our registration office at (928) 555-0170.
Or register online at http://www.macycc.edu/registration/register2.html.

Learn to Use Your Computer More Efficiently

Hands-On Classes ◆ Earn 1 credit Hour

Macy Community College
Computer Learning Center

OFTC 110 Keyboarding on the Job

This course builds competencies needed in today's electronic offices: speed, accuracy, and production of various types of business correspondence, forms, and reports.
August 22–October 31
Mondays 2:00–1:50

OFTC 111 Building Speed and Accuracy

This class is designed to improve keyboarding speed and accuracy through timed copy analysis, goal setting, and corrective drill practice.
August 23–October 25
Tuesdays 11:00–11:50

OFTC 112 Using Microsoft® Office

This course provides an introduction to Microsoft® Office and its popular word processing, spreadsheet, presentations, information management, and database software.
August 22–October 13
Mondays 10:00–10:50

OFTC 113 Word Processing

This class covers basic word processing functions. Learn to enter and edit text, format documents, print files, and save your work.
August 23–October 25
Tuesdays 1:00–1:50

These are beginning computer courses. No prerequisite is required.

MACY COMMUNITY COLLEGE   415 W. Beale St., Kingman, AZ 86401-5705
To enroll, contact our registration office at (928) 555-0170.
Or register online at http://www.macycc.edu/registration/register2.html .

Activity 2-3: Check a Flyer Against a Calendar

1 Open *Balloonfest* from your student data disk. Save a copy of this file as *Act2-3[your initials]* (for example, *Act2-3el*) and print it.

2 Check the information in the flyer against the calendar below. Apply proofreaders' marks to any errors you find in the flyer. Correct the flyer and print it again.

3 Proofread the corrected flyer, following the proofreading steps on page 2.

	Friday, August 24		Saturday, August 25		Sunday, August 26
2pm	Food Booths (to 10 p.m.)	6am	Late registration, 5K Run	6am	Food Booths (to 10 p.m.)
300	Craft Fair (to 10 p.m.)	700	Hudelson 5K Run	700	Craft Fair (to 5 p.m.)
400	Balloons Enter the Park	800	Craft Fair (to 10 p.m.)	800	Folk Music (to 9 a.m.)
500	Balloon Race	900	Food Booths (to 10 p.m.)	900	NASCAR Simulator (to 6 p.m.)
630	Blue Moon Band (Main Stage, to 9 p.m.)	1000	Children's Activity Area (to 5 p.m.)	1000	Balloon Race
		2pm	Balloon Race	2pm	Cardboard Boat Race
900	Laser Light Show (1 hr.)	400	Band TBA (Main Stage, to 6 p.m.)	300	Children's Activity Area (to 5 p.m.)
		730	Balloon Glow	500	Balloon Race
				900	Fireworks Display (to 9:30)

Activity 2-4: Proofread a News Release Against Marked-Up Copy

1 Open *FBLA Release* from the student data disk. This file is a corrected copy of the marked-up news release on the next page. Save the file as *Act2-4[your initials]* (for example, *Act2-4el*) and print it.

2 Proofread the printout by comparing it to the marked-up copy to make sure that all corrections were made and that no new errors were introduced. Using proofreaders' marks, mark any errors you find on the printout.

3 Correct the errors and print a clean copy. Proofread this copy, not against the marked-up copy this time, following the steps for proofreading on page 2.

Amiscot High School
1200 Est King Avenue
Kingsville, Tx 7836-593

(361) 555-0153　*12 pt*　　　　　　　　　　**mjames@amiscot.net**　*12 pt*

NEWS RELEASE　　　　　　　　　　　　　　　　　Contact Person: Mary James
March 27, 200-
For Release: immediately

AMISCOT HIGH STUDENTS ATTEND FBLA CONFERENCE

KINGSVILLE, TX—Future Busines Leaders of America member representing Amiscot High School attended the Texis State FBLA Leadership conference March 25 and 26 in in DAllas.

A total of 902 student and advisors from 80 Chapters statewide attended the thevent. Amiscot High School sent 17 student and two faculty mmbers the conference.

The Conference included activities in personal development and business training.

Students participated in competitive events including accounting, parliamentary procedure, entrepreneurship, job interviews, and public speaking. An awards luncheon ended the annual conference. ~~An awards luncheon ended the annual conference.~~

Winnrs from AHS included Nancy Hinrich and Norton Trish, battle of the chapters team, first place; Nicol Fisg, keyboarding applications, sixth place; Behn Sheth, impromptu speak, seventh place; TomTully, business law 8th place; and Keven Stephens, information processing, 9th place.

Faculty mmbers from AHS attending the conference were Mary and Carol Foster, FBL advisors.

FBLA is a national Organization that promotes business leadership training. *for high school students*

###

Activity 2-5: **Check a Memo Against a Phone List**

Proofread the following memo. Mark all keyboarding errors with proofreaders' marks. You have a partial list of residents of Greenville on your student data disk (*Greenville Phone Directory*). Check the names, addresses, and phone numbers in the memo against this directory.

Can you think of a more useful order in which names could be arranged? If so, write a note on the copy for the keyboardist.

 Greenville Community Arts Club

TO: The Membershp

FROM: Michi Harada, President

DATE: June 8, 200-

SUBJECT: Members Left Out of Directory

The following ninety members (all residents of Greenville) were mistakenly left out of

our new directory. Pleawse add them to the membership roster and double-check names

and addresses for accuracy.

Member	Address	ZIP Code	Phone No.
Aaron, James, Jr.	10 Mcallister Street	38701-4213	555-0198
Adams, Anna	899 Campbell Rd	38701-4118	555-0183
Alexander, Letitia.	423 Weatherbee Street	38701-6364	555-010
Alexander, Beatrice	86 Cannon Street	38701-5919	555-0146
ALlen, Edith	733 S. Dyer Circle	38701-6469	555-0137
Allen, Carol	591 Palemmo Street	38701-3113	555-0183
Allen, Chasity	506 Byrd Drive	38701-5740	555-0121-
Andersen, Kenneth W.	3039 E. Read Road	38703-9542	555-0163
Aderholt, dwight	1123 S. Raeway Road	38703-8246	555-0122
Alexander, Letitia	423 Wetherbee Street	38701-6362	555-0101

Proofread Numbers

Everyone has had the experience of being charged the wrong price for a purchase. How do these errors happen?

Many stores use electronic scanners to read the price of an item at the checkout counter. These scanners are linked to a computer that reads the Universal Product Code (UPC) on the product or tag and compares it to the price that was entered into the store's computer. Errors result when store employees enter an incorrect price or fail to change the price to reflect a sale (or price increase). These errors are costly to consumers. They may also result in a fine for the company.

Making Sure the Numbers Add Up

Making sure numbers are correct is important. Proofreading numbers involves inspecting a document for errors in amounts, extensions, percentages, telephone numbers, Social Security numbers, addresses, dates, and other numbers.

Numbers that have been keyed from another source lend themselves to transposition errors. Transpositions in numbers are often harder to detect than those in words. For example, in the word *Illinosi*, it is easy to see that the *s* and the *i* have been transposed. In the ZIP Code 62810-1419, however, it is not obvious that the *01* has been incorrectly keyed as *10*.

Numbers keyed incorrectly are costly to businesses. Misaddressed packages will not be delivered. Incorrect phone numbers will lead to the wrong people. Misdialed fax numbers will send the wrong person the information. Inaccurate numbers on invoices may result in paying less than what is owed or in angry customers.

© GettyImages/PhotoDisc

Numbers must be checked carefully.

Preparing to Proofread Numbers

When you are proofreading, you should check all numbers except those that you know are correct. For example, important dates should be checked against a calendar. Phone numbers and addresses should be compared to a current phone directory or database. Prices should be verified against a price list. Calculations should be checked twice with a calculator.

Before you begin proofreading a document with numbers, collect the information and tools you will need. Remember that a calculator is always available on your computer. If certain numbers are used throughout the document, write them on a separate piece of paper so you can check them easily.

The Internet is useful for checking numbers. For example, the best place to check ZIP Codes is at the United States Postal Service Web site, at http://www.usps.com. If a document lists a temperature in Celsius and Fahrenheit or a weight in kilograms and pounds, you can use an online conversion calculator to check whether the conversion was done correctly.

Proofreading Tips

The following tips will help you when you are proofreading numbers:

> Read numbers in groups. For example, the telephone number 618-555-0123 can be read in three parts: *six-one-eight*, *five-five-five*, *zero-one-two-three*. This is called **chunking**.

> Read numbers aloud.

> Read numbers from right to left instead of left to right.

> Proofread numbers with a partner, one of you reading to the other.

> When you are checking the addition of long columns of numbers, add them once from top to bottom and the second time from bottom to top.

> Use a calculator.

> Before checking a total, estimate it in your head. Then calculate the answer and compare it to your estimate. Does your answer make sense?

Activity 3-1: Check a Check Register

At the start of February, Carol had a balance of $2,855.78 in her checking account. After writing a check, Carol subtracts the amount of the check from the balance to obtain her new balance. When she makes a deposit, Carol adds the amount of the deposit to the balance. Proofread Carol's check register for math errors. Apply proofreaders' marks as needed to correct the running balance.

Number	Date	Description of Transaction	Payment/ Debit	Deposit/ Credit	Balance
					$ 2,855.78
1685	2/6	Chicago Power Co.	365.83		2,490.95
1686	2/6	Tower Savings and Loan	942.85		1,548.10
1687	2/6	Frank Lin Insurance	159.00		1,389.00
1688	2/7	Kendall Cleaners	10.50		1,379.50
1689	2/7	Vandegall Securities	200.00		1,179.50
Dep.	2/10	Salary		1,500	2,879.50
——	2/11	Cash (ATM)	100.00		2,779.50

Number	Date	Description of Transaction	Payment/ Debit	Deposit/ Credit	Balance
					$ 2,779.50
1690	2/11	American Phone	86.00		2,693.50
1691	2/11	Community Cable	30.00		2,663.50
1692	2/11	Beacon Food Mart	180.00		2,483.50
1693	2/12	Prospect Business College	690.00		2,793.50
1694	2/12	United Way	50.00		2,743.50
1695	2/12	Mason's	89.90		2,653.50
1696	2/15	Mike's Internet	25.00		2,668.50

Activity 3-2: Check Invoices Against a Price List

Check the invoices on the next page against the price list below. Be sure to check all calculations. An $8.95 delivery fee is added to all orders. The sales tax is 8.75 percent, and it is applied to the items sold and not to the delivery fee. Apply proofreaders' marks to any errors you find in the invoices. You will find errors in numbers and in keyboarding.

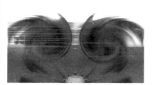

WINDY CITY FLORISTS

1500 W. Lake St. 🕊 *Chicago, IL 60607-1406*
(312) 555-0127 🕊 *http://www.windycityflorists.com*

PRICE LIST   AUGUST 200–

Item	Description	Price
Assorted tulips	Dozen tulips, assorted colors, clear glass vase	$44.95
Autumn welcome	Orange Asiatic lily, assorted fall flowers, glass pedestal bowl	$64.95
Balloon & flowers	Mylar balloon w/mixed autumn arrangement, clear glass vase	$44.50
Desk garden	Variegated ivy, fern, diffenbachia, and African violet in ceramic dish	$44.95
Dozen pink roses	Dozen long-stemmed pink roses, crystal vase	$75.00
Dozen red roses	Dozen long-stemmed red roses, crystal vase	$75.00
Dozen yellow roses	Dozen long-stemmed yellow roses, crystal vase	$75.00
Everyday cheers	Yellow roses and white daisies in a yellow mug	$30.95
Favorite hello	Carnations and larkspur w/baby harp seal stuffed animal	$30.95
Gourmet tin	Assorted gourmet chocolates and cookies in seasonal tin	$49.95
Organic fruits	2 grapefruit, 6 oranges, 6 apples, 1 bunch grapes, 4 kiwis	$50.00
Peaceful garden	Bromeliad, Chinese evergreen, croton	$75.00
Plant & fruit basket	Kalanch, apples, pears, bananas, grapes, long wicker basket	$75.00
White roses & lilies	Ten white roses and lilies w/stock, clear glass vase	$49.95

Windy City Florists

1500 W. Lake St. ✿ Chicago, IL 60607-1406
(312) 555-0127 ✿ http://www.windycityflorists.com

To: CQS Corporation
15 S. Throop St.
Chicago, IL 60607-2517

Invoice No: 2801
Date: 8/30

Quantity	Item	Unit Price	Amount
2	Gourmet tins	49.95	99.90
3	Balloon & flowers	49.95	149.85
		Subtotal	$249.75
		Delivery Fee	8.95
		Sales Tax	21.85
		Total Due	$280.55

Windy City Florists

1500 W. Lake St. ✿ Chicago, IL 60607-1406
(312) 555-0127 ✿ http://www.windycityflorists.com

To: Ms. Alice Chiang
98 W. 19th St.
Chicago, IL 60616-1633

Invoice No: 2802
Date: 8/30

Quantity	Item	Unit Price	Amount
2	Dozen red roses	75.00	75.00
1	Assorted tulips	44.95	44.95
		Subtotal	$119.95
		Delivery Fee	8.95
		Sales Tax	10.50
		Total Due	$139.40

Windy City Florists

1500 W. Lake St. ✿ Chicago, IL 60607-1406
(312) 555-0127 ✿ http://www.windycityflorists.com

To: Multiflex Media
203 S. Loomis St.
Chicago, IL 60607-2896

Invoice No: 2803
Date: 8/30

Quantity	Item	Unit Price	Amount
2	Favorite hello	30.95	61.90
1	Peaceful garden	75.00	75.00
1	Desk garden	44.95	44.95
		Subtotal	$151.85
		Delivery Fee	8.95
		Sales Tax	13.29
		Total Due	$174.09

Windy City Florists

1500 W. Lake St. ✿ Chicago, IL 60607-1406
(312) 555-0127 ✿ http://www.windycityflorists.com

To: N. P. Forsyth & Co.
49 W. Throop St.
Chicago, IL 60605-2089

Invoice No: 2804
Date: 8/30

Quantity	Item	Unit Price	Amount
1	Autumn welcome	64.95	64.95
1	Plan & fruit	75.00	75.00
		Subtotal	$139.95
		Delivery Fee	8.95
		Sales Tax	13.03
		Total Due	$161.93

Activity 3-3: **Check a Monthly Report Against Receipts**

1 The daily receipts of Dog and Suds Salon for Pampered Pups have been copied from the calendar below for the April monthly report on the next page. Check to see if the figures have been copied and totaled correctly. Apply proofreaders' marks to any errors you find in the report.

2 Open the data disk file *04 Monthly Receipts* and save it as *Act3-3si* (replace *si* with your initials). This file contains the monthly report that appears on the next page. Make the corrections you marked to this file. Turn in both the marked-up copy and your final corrected copy.

April 200–						
Sunday	Monday	Tuesday	Wednesday	Thursday	Friday	Saturday
					1 $870.50	2 $558.50
3	4	5 $684.50	6 $684.50	7 $778.75	8 $900.45	9 $556.45
10	11	12 $684.50	13 $454.54	14 $565.80	15 $725.90	16 $1,000.65
17	18	19 $665.50	20 $888.50	21 $555.90	22 $455.50	23 $444.50
24	25	26 $575.25	27 $668.50	28 $674.50	29 $444.50	30 $887.50

DOG AND SUDS

SALON FOR PAMPERED PUPS

DAILY RECEIPTS
APRIL 200–

Week of	Tuesday	Wednesday	Thursday	Friday	Saturday	Totals
April 1–2					$870.50	$558.50
April 3–9	$648.50	$684.50	$778.75	$900.54	$556.45	$3,568.74
April 10–16	$648.50	$454.54	$565.80	$725.90	$10,000.65	$12,395.39
April 17–23	$665.60	$888.50	$555.90	$455.50	$444.50	$3,010.00
April 24–30	$575.50	$668.50	$674.50	$444.55	$887.50	$3,250.50
Totals		$1,678.04	$2,574.95	$2,526.49		$22,783.13

Activity 3-4: Compare a Registration List to Cards

1 Open the data disk file *Registration List*, save it as *Act3-4si* (replace *si* with your initials), and print it.

2 Proofread the registration list against the registration cards below. Apply proofreaders' marks to any errors you find in the registration list. You will find errors in numbers and in keyboarding.

3 Make any needed corrections, and turn in your final corrected copy.

Name: Max Dyker
Title: Principal
School: South Seattle High
Address: 7300 Greenwood Ave. N.
Seattle, WA 98103-5042
Phone: (206) 555-0154
Fax: (206) 555-0155
E-mail: mdyker@washingtoned.net
Payment: Check ☐   Credit Card ☑   P.O. ☐

Name: Robert Hosbrook
Title: Principal
School: Haines City District #101
Address: 509 E. Hinson Ave.
Haines City, FL 33844-5239
Phone: (863) 555-0111
Fax: (863) 555-0112
E-mail: rhosbrook@hcd.hs.us
Payment: Check ☐   Credit Card ☑   P.O. ☐

Name: Sandy Klein
Title: Dean of Students
School: Barwick Country Day School
Address: 2050 E. Main St.
Barwick, GA 31720-2000
Phone: (912) 555-0183
Fax: (912) 555-0130
E-mail: sklein@bcds.net
Payment: Check ☐   Credit Card ☑   P.O. ☐

Name: Keith Newcomb
Title: Assistant Principal
School: Chidrow High School
Address: 6420 Main St.
Bonners Ferry, ID 83805-8520
Phone: 208-555-0110
Fax:
E-mail:
Payment: Check ☐   Credit Card ☐   P.O. ☑

Name: Mary O'Laughlin
Title: Assistant Principal
School: Pittsburgh East High School
Address: 524 Grant St.
Pittsburgh, PA 15219-2501
Phone: (412) 555-0105
Fax: (412) 555-0106
E-mail: mjo.pittsburgheast.net
Payment: Check ☑   Credit Card ☐   P.O. ☐

Name: Theresa Ramirez
Title: Vice Principal
School: Fayette/Bond High School
Address: 900 N.W. Garfield Ave.
Corvallis, OR 97330-2116
Phone: 541-555-0109
Fax: 541-555-0199
E-mail: tlramirez@fb.hs.us
Payment: Check ☑   Credit Card ☐   P.O. ☐

Activity 3-5: Compare a Report to Expense Slips

1 Open the data disk file *Travel Expense Report 12*, save it as *Act3-5si* (replace *si* with your initials), and print it.

2 Proofread the report against the expense slips below. Apply proofreaders' marks to any errors you find in the report. You will find errors in numbers and in keyboarding.

3 Make any needed corrections, and turn in your final corrected copy.

Name ___John Jackson___

Employee I.D. ___12-0415___

Expense Report for Week Ending ___03/19___

Destination ___San Jose___

Mileage _____

Meals ___123___ Hotel ___280___

Plane/Train ___462___

Car Rental ___171___ Parking ___35___

Misc. Please List _____

Signed ___John Jackson___

Name ___Roger Norton___

Employee I.D. ___33-0821___

Expense Report for Week Ending ___03/19___

Destination ___Salt Lake City___

Mileage _____

Meals ___$135.00___ Hotel ___$277.00___

Plane/Train ___$787.00___

Car Rental ___$158.00___ Parking ___$40.00___

Misc. Please List _____

Signed ___Roger Norton___

Name ___Nancy Cartwright___

Employee I.D. ___12-1419___

Expense Report for Week Ending ___03/19___

Destination ___Chicago___

Mileage ___$178.20___

Meals ___$129.00___ Hotel ___$258.00___

Plane/Train _____

Car Rental _____ Parking ___$42.00___

Misc. Please List _____

Signed ___Nancy Cartwright___

Name ___Imogene McDonal___

Employee I.D. ___22-8989___

Expense Report for Week Ending ___March 19___

Destination ___Minneapolis___

Mileage _____

Meals ___120___ Hotel ___269___

Plane/Train ___375___

Car Rental ___153___ Parking ___30___

Misc. Please List _____

Signed ___Imogene McDonal___

INTERNET

Activity 3-6: Check ZIP Codes

Go to the United States Postal Service Web site at http://www.usps.com. Check the ZIP Codes in the following addresses for errors. Apply proofreaders' marks to any errors you find.

Clevenger, Arthur (Mr.)
1609 Atherton Wa y
Salinas, CA 93096-3106

Elkins, Bernard (Mr.)
14 Arrowhead Rd.
Leominster, MA 01453-4580

Jen, Ai-lien (Ms.)
759 Westview Ave.
Athens, AL 36511

Lombardo, Patrick (Mr.)
8539 Bells Mill Rd.
Potomac, MD 20854-072

Madenda, Camilla (Ms.)
1500 S. Arizona Ave.
Yuma, AZ 85364-4771

Matthews, Bonita (Mrs.)
3210 Thousand Oaks Dr.
Louisville, KY 41250-2703

Ramirez, Julio (Dr.)
5910 Sixta Dr.
El Paso, TX 70032-2315

Walker, Charlene (Ms.)
500 N. Broadway
Billings, MT 59101-1116

Proofread Numbers

Use the Spelling Checker

FOCUS

Spellbound

> I have a spelling checker,
> It came with by PC;
> It plainly marks four my revue
> Mistakes I cannot sea
> I've run this poem threw it,
> I'm sure your please to no,
> Its letter perfect in it's weigh,
> My checker tolled me sew.
> —Author unknown

Spelling Checker Features

Recognizing misspelled and misused words is critical. These words are embarrassing to the writer and distracting to the reader. Proofreading involves using your word processor's spelling checker and then examining the document for errors the spelling checker did not detect.

You can spell-check all of a document or selected text. You can set the feature to check automatically as you key or all at once when you select the spelling option.

The spelling checker compares your document to words in its dictionary. If a word is not in its dictionary, the spelling checker will mark the word as a possible error. If the feature is checking as you key, you can right-click the marked word for a pop-up menu that suggests spellings and offers options. If you are running a check all at once, a dialog box shows the suggested changes and more options. The options and their exact names vary, but they usually include the following:

Option	Result
Ignore or Ignore Once	The spelling checker ignores the word and moves to the next word.
Ignore All	The spelling checker ignores the word throughout the document.
Add or Add to Dictionary	The spelling checker adds the word to its dictionary and will accept it as correct for any document.
Change	The spelling checker changes the word to the suggested spelling you chose or the correction you keyed.
Change All	The spelling checker makes the correction throughout the document.
Resume	The spelling checker starts checking again after you have edited a word.
AutoCorrect	The spelling checker adds the misspelled word and the proper spelling to its AutoCorrect list.

The AutoCorrect feature corrects common keying errors automatically as you key. For example, you might key *teh* by mistake and find it changed to *the*. If you frequently make a particular keying error, you can add the error to the AutoCorrect feature.

In Microsoft® Word, the spelling checker is usually run together with the grammar checker. Other types of software also have spelling checkers. For instance, most e-mail programs have a spell-check feature. It is often not as good as the spelling checker in word processing software. If you are writing a long e-mail, it is better to draft it in word processing software, run the spelling checker, and then paste it into the e-mail.

Working With Spelling Checkers

You should be aware of the limits of spelling checkers. Older versions, for example, are less likely to recognize new terms. Any spelling checker is limited in the number of words it contains. It will not include as many words as a print dictionary. Some spelling checkers offer specialized dictionaries (of medical or legal terms, for example). Generally, a spelling checker will not find the following types of errors:

Type of Error	Example
Incorrect choice of words	*There* office is down the hall.
Words not in its dictionary	*miskeyed, kerfuffle*
Words that should have a hyphen	*know how* instead of *know-how*
Two words when one is correct	*past time* instead of *pastime*
Proper names misspelled	*Brown* for *Browne; John* for *Jon*
Incorrect words resulting from keying errors	*hair* miskeyed as *air*
Specialized vocabulary	*ototoxic*

Run the spelling checker after you have finished a document, just before proofreading it. If you make more than a few changes, run the spelling checker again.

When the spelling checker flags a word and offers you a list of suggested replacements, carefully read the words and do not simply pick the first one. Many times, the first one is the correct word, but sometimes it is not. If the beginning of the word is spelled incorrectly, the spelling checker may not be able to find the word. You may have to enter the first characters of the word in the document to find it.

As you can see, even with the best spelling checker, you need a good dictionary. Proofreaders should have at least one print dictionary on hand. Many dictionaries are available online. For example, Merriam-Webster offers a good general dictionary at http://www.m-w.com. The dictionary will pronounce the word for you. Other online dictionaries can be found with a search for *online dictionary* in Google or another search engine.

Although the electronic spelling checker is an extraordinary tool, it is not intended to replace the experienced proofreader. The spelling checker is a proofreading aid, but it is not a substitute for the proofreader's keen eyes and sharp mind. Remember, *you* are the final proofreader.

Activity 4-1: Spelling Checker Stumpers

Each of the following sentences contains a word that is commonly confused with a similar-sounding word. Find the errors and use proofreaders' marks to correct them. A list of commonly confused words appears in the *Mechanics* file in the Reference Guide folder on your student data disk.

1　The account is 60 days passed due.

2　The Mesa Verde project can precede next week.

3　Savings bonds maybe a good long-term investment.

4　I'm looking forward to you're visit.

5　We will be using the second addition of *Office Management Made Easy*.

6　Please do not altar the floral arrangement.

7　The group will meet on the west steps of the Capital in Des Moines.

8　The delegates took a ten-minute brake between meetings.

9　We went threw the side door to enter the house.

10　Listen to your radio for school closings based on inclement whether.

Activity 4-2: Spell-Check a Paragraph

1　Key the following paragraph exactly as is and save it as *Act4-2si*.

2　Spell-check the paragraph, making corrections as needed.

3　Proofread the paragraph. Watch for errors that your spelling checker may have missed.

4　Make any needed corrections, and turn in your final corrected copy.

When Sue turned in her reprt, she felt confidant that the spelling checker had found all her heirs. Sue had witten hear report on nursing. She was going to school to to get her associate's degree in nursing, or ADN. When Sue got her [aper back, she was dismayed to find that she had recieved a C. The paper contained several errors that her spelling checker did not find. The instuctor told her to us an online or plint dictionary. Some of her errors were medical terms that were not in the software's dictionary. Sue began too look up words in the dictionary and to proof read carefully. She used both a medical and a general dictionary. On the rest of her papers, Sue recieved a grade of B or better.

Activity 4-3: **Check Spelling in a Letter**

1 Open the data disk file *Hoerning* and save it as *Act4-3si*.

2 Make the corrections indicated in the marked-up copy below.

3 Run the spelling checker, making corrections as needed.

4 Proofread the document. Watch for errors that your spelling checker may have missed.

5 Make any needed corrections, and turn in your final corrected copy.

Tunney Software   151 Powell St.   San Francisco CA 94102-2203
http://www.tunneysoftware.com   (415) 555-0187

August 11, 200-

Mr. Brad Hoerning, President
Hoerning Corporation
5904 Fountain Avenue
Los Angeles, CA 90028-8046

Dear Mr. Hoerning:

major

Each year, Hoerning Coporation employees travel to dozens of cities around the world. Imagine an employee who is visiting Buenos Aires for the first time. She steps form a taxi and checks her location onher mobile phone. She waves the phone at a restaurant and instantly gets a menu, translated into English. She sees a beautiful public garden across the street, waves it again, and gets a full description, with an offer for an audio tour. Hotels, restaurants, major businesses, banks, transportation, shopping, tourist sites—they are all ways at her fingertips. That is what our Friendly Presence software has to offer.

SP

Friendly Presence serves 75% of foreign cities in which Hoerning Corporation does business. Our phones use GPS technology and custom finder an navigation applications. Friendly Presence takes care of the details, leaving your employees free to take care of business.

May we meet with you to show you how Friendly Presence can save Hoerning Corporation time, money, and effort? Our sales representative will call net week to arrange a meeting.

Thank you for your consideration.

Sincerely

Calvin Tunney

pt

Enclosures

Activity 4-4: **Spell-Check and Proofread a Report**

1 Open the data disk file *Communication Skills* and save it as *Act4-4si*.

2 Run the spelling checker, making corrections as needed.

3 Proofread the document. Watch for errors that your spelling checker may have missed.

4 Make any needed corrections, and turn in your final corrected copy.

Activity 4-5: **Spell-Check and Proofread Newsletter Articles**

1 Open the data disk files *Presidential News*, *Leadership Conference*, and *Officers*. Save the files as *Act4-5Asi*, *Act4-5Bsi*, and *Act4-5Csi*.

2 Check these newsletter articles against the reporters' notes below. Make any corrections as needed to the articles.

3 Run the spelling checker, making corrections as needed. Do not correct uses of the passive voice.

4 Proofread the documents. Watch for errors that your spelling checker may have missed.

5 Make any needed corrections, and turn in your final corrected copy.

Barb Britton, Pres., 555-0126

V.P. James Cude, 555-0124

Recording Sec'y, Mike Garrison, 555-0122

Susan Tiemann, Corresponding Sec'y, 555-0120

Roger Telford, Treasurer, 555-0121

—**Mary Ann Widener**
Volunteer of the Year

—**Ann Castorini**
Chapel restoration
project

COC Leadership Conference—6/13 & 14, Crown Plaza, Springfield

→ *"Valuing Diversity," workshops*

→ *carpool from Pacey's parking lot, 6:30 a.m. each day*

Activity 4-6: Get Help with Confusing Words

Go to http://www.confusingwords.com. Look up three words that are confusing to you and write a short paragraph about each one. Save your file as *Act4-6si*.

Activity 4-7: Proofread a Legal Decision

1 Open the data disk file *Roberts Add* and save it as *Act4-7si*.

2 This document is a paragraph that will be added to a legal decision. Check the paragraph against the list of legal terms and guidelines below. Make any corrections as needed to the paragraph.

3 Run the spelling checker, making corrections as needed. Do not change the verb use.

4 Proofread the document. Watch for errors that your spelling checker may have missed.

5 Make any needed corrections, and turn in your final corrected copy.

> ➔ *appellant*
> ➔ *de novo*   *Passive voice is OK.*
> ➔ *prima facie*
> ➔ *warrantless*   *Don't use italics.*
> ➔ *writ of habeas corpus*

Activity 4-8: Proofread an E-Mail

1 Open the data disk file *Rummage Sale* and save it as *Act4-8si*. If you have e-mail software in your classroom, copy the text of the document into your e-mail software.

2 Run the spelling checker, making corrections as needed. If you are using classroom e-mail software, use the e-mail software's spelling checker. Do not correct uses of the passive voice.

3 Proofread the document. Watch for errors that your spelling checker may have missed.

4 Make any needed corrections, and turn in your final corrected copy. If you are using e-mail software, send the e-mail to your instructor.

Team Proofreading

FOCUS

Mistakes in credit reports can ruin the financial standing of hardworking Americans. One in four credit reports has errors serious enough to bar consumers from buying a home, opening a bank account, or getting a job—and many contain mistakes of some kind, according to a survey released in 2004 by U.S. PIRG, a consumer group.*

What Is Team Proofreading?

Team proofreading requires two or more persons. One person reads the draft or original copy aloud, while another person follows along and marks the other copy. Sometimes one person proofreads the copy and then passes it to one or more others, who also proofread it.

Team proofreading is especially effective when checking the accuracy of technical copy, long lists, unfamiliar terms, names, and numbers. It is useful for the following:

> Annual reports

> Technical reports

> Legal briefs

> Medical histories

> Documents containing foreign words

Team proofreading helps with frequently used documents. Errors in such documents waste people's time and can cause mistakes, annoyance, and lost sales. Frequently used documents include the following:

> Address lists

> Phone lists

> E-mail lists

> Price lists

> Policy and procedures manuals

> Catalogs

> **Intranet** and Internet documents (An intranet is an Internet-like company network.)

Documents with a Large Audience

Documents that will be reproduced and distributed to many people merit team proofreading. Though every communication sent to others requires careful proofreading,

---

* Executive Summary, "Mistakes Do Happen: A Look at Errors in Consumer Credit Reports," National Association of State PIRGs, June 2004, http://uspirg.org/uspirg.asp?id2=13649&id3=USPIRG&#1, 13 August 2004.

keeping embarrassing errors out of text that will be distributed to many people is especially important. An error found after a printer has made 5,000 copies of a document is an expensive error. A newspaper advertisement with the wrong sale price can cost customer goodwill and business. Documents that are often distributed to a large audience include the following:

> Newspaper advertisements
> Mail merge letters and other mass mailings
> Web pages
> Newsletters

Teams may share proofreading responsibilities.

Documents Produced with Special Technologies

Documents produced with special technologies may contain unexpected or unusual errors and should always be proofread carefully. These technologies include scanning, voice recognition software, and document conversion.

Scanners are machines that read paper copy and create computer files from it. Scanners sometimes misread text. A scanner may read the letter *I*, for example, as *1*, *L*, or even *%*. The quality of a computer file produced from scanned material often depends on the quality of the original copy. A smudged paper copy, for instance, is more likely to be misread. In addition, scanning software must be trained to recognize the characters of different type fonts. Before this training is complete, errors are more likely.

Voice recognition software produces keyed text from spoken words. People must train voice recognition software to recognize their particular speech patterns. Especially during this training period, the software may incorrectly translate what a speaker says. It may "hear" *next time I see you* as *next to my see you*, for example.

Documents scanned or converted from other software can contain errors resulting from the conversion, such as odd characters or long strings of characters. Scanning and file conversion can also strip formatting from the file.

Documents produced with special technologies include the following:

> Scanned documents
> Documents created with voice recognition software
> Documents converted from other software or formats

Original Work

We are more likely to miss errors in documents we compose and key ourselves. It is easier to see the mistakes of others than our own. We read what we think we said, instead of what we did say. When we are keying work others have written, we are less likely to detect errors when we are not well versed in the meaning of the text. Original work suitable for team proofreading includes the following:

> Documents we compose ourselves
> Documents keyed from handwritten notes

Activity 5-1: Proofread Foreign Terms in a Team

The following Spanish vocabulary list has been started for you on your data disk. The format is in place; you need to enter words 6–20.

1 Open the data disk file *Vocab3* and save it as *Act5-1si*.

2 To the right of the number 6, key *informe anual*. Then press Tab, key *annual report*, and press Enter.

3 Key the remaining words in the same way. To insert the letter *ó* with its accent mark in *nómina*, key Alt + 0243 using the numeric keypad. If the special character is not supported by your software, you can draw the mark on the *o* in the printed copy.

4 Proofread your list with a teammate. One person should read aloud while the other checks the copy, marking errors with proofreaders' marks.

5 Make any needed corrections, and turn in your final corrected copy.

VOCABULARY LIST Week 3			
Term	Definition	Term	Definition
a menudo	often	mediano	medium, average
curriculum vitae	resume	mimado	spoiled
entrevista de trabajo	job interview	mojado	wet
factura	invoice	moreno	brunet, tan
gratis	free	nómina de pago	payroll
informe anual	annual report	nublado	cloudy
ligero	light (in weight)	opuesto	opposite
liso	smooth	orden de pedido	purchase order
listo	ready, clever	peinado	comb or combed
lleno	full	solicitud de trabajo	job application

Activity 5-2: Revise a List and Proofread in a Team

The vocabulary list you keyed in Activity 5-1 has been updated for Week 4.

1 Open *Act5-1si* and save it as *Act5-2si*.

2 Update the list as shown below.

3 Alphabetize the list (select the numbered list, but not "Vocabulary List/Week 4," and use the Table/Sort feature).

4 Proofread your list with a teammate. One person should read aloud while the other checks the copy, marking errors with proofreaders' marks.

5 Make any needed corrections, and turn in your final corrected copy.

VOCABULARY LIST Week 4			
Term	Definition	Term	Definition
a menudo	often	mediano	medium, average
curriculum vitae	resume	la tarea	task, homework
entrevista de trabajo	job interview	el rumbo	direction, road
factura	invoice	el riesgo	risk
dinero	money	nómina de pago	payroll
informe anual	annual report	el sonido	sound
el plazo	period of time	opuesto	opposite
la red	net, network	orden de pedido	purchase order
el resumen	summary	el saludo	greeting
el retrato	picture, portrait	solicitud de trabajo	job application

Activity 5-3: Proofread a Manual File in a Team

The list of abbreviations on the next page is intended for a law office's style manual.

1 Open the data disk file *Abbreviations* and save it as *Act5-3si*.

2 Use team proofreading to check the file against the copy on the next page. Apply proofreaders' marks to any errors you find in the file.

3 Make any needed corrections, and turn in your final corrected copy.

COMMON LEGAL ABBREVIATIONS

A.D.
  in the year of [our] Lord (L., *anno Domini*)
Atty.
  Attorney
B/L, b/l
  bill of lading
d.b.a.
  doing business as
Esq.
  Esquire
et al.
  and others (L., *et alii*)
et seq.
  and the following (L., *et sequentes*)

f.k.a.
  formerly known as
f.o.b./FOB
  free on board
id., idem
  the same (L., *idem*)
J.D.
  Doctor of Jurisprudence (L., *juris doctor*)
L.L.C.
  limited liability corporation
Messrs.
  plural of *Mr.* (F., *Messieurs*)
P.C.
  professional corporation

Activity 5-4: Proofread a Newspaper Advertisement in a Team

1 Open the data disk file *104275* and save it as *Act5-4si*.

2 Use team proofreading to check for errors in the newspaper advertisement below. The data disk file contains the correct ad copy information. Apply proofreaders' marks to the advertisement, and initial a printout of the data disk file in the space provided. Each team member should sign off on the data disk file after proofreading the advertisement.

CIVIL ENGINNER

We are looking for experienced, multi-skilled engineers to join our successful team. Focus on transportation and public works design. BSE or MSCE and 20+ yers of engineering experience required. Must have EIT or PET registration and MicroStation, InRoads, GEOPACK, and/or Autocad skills. Experience designing highways, light rail, or transportation highly desirable. Must have excellent communication, intepersonal, and problem-solving skills.

Competive salary and comprehensive benefits to include flexible working hours, medical, dental, optical, and professional fees. Send resume by 8/8/0- to Personnel Dept., Tawanda Corporation, 5800 Kirkpatrick Blvd., Houston, TX 77028-3394, or apply online at http://tawandacorp.com. No phone calls, please.

Activity 5-5: Proofread Web Page Copy in a Team

1 Open the data disk file *848320* and save it as *Act5-5si*.

2 Use team proofreading to check the Web page copy against the information below. Apply proofreaders' marks to any errors you find in the Web page copy.

3 Make any needed corrections, and turn in your final corrected copy.

Jasper Real Estate   802 W. Main St. | Salem, IL 62881-1407 | (618) 555-0100

1302 Hawthorn Rd   Price: $229,900

Gorgeous home, great neighborhood!

Beautiful landscaped lot. 3 BR, 3 BA, huge LR

w/fireplace. Formal DR, office/dem. Large,

eat-in kitchen. Beautiful open foyer w/oak

stairway. Extra-large garage, separate

workshop, tiered deck, pool

© Comstock Images

Rooms	Size	Floors	Walls	Other Information
BR 1	16 x 13.5	Carpet	Paper	Ceiling fan, walk-in closet
BR 2	13.5 x 14	Carpet	Solid wood	Walk-in closet
BR 3	10.5 x 10	Carpet	Paper	Double closet
Foyer	15 x 12	Wood	Paper	Coat closet & storage, oak stairway
LR	30 x 15	Carpet	Paper	Fireplace, ceiling fan, leaded glass windows
DR	18 x 15	Carpet	Paper / wood	Chandelier
K/D	14 x 20	Carpet	Paper	Custom cabinets w/special features
BA 1	7.5 x 5.5	Carpet	Paper	Enclosed tub/shower, vanity, linen closet
BA 2	5 x 6.5	Carpet	Paper / wood	Stool, vanity, shower
BA 3	10 x 5	Carpet	Paper	Enclosed tub/shower, linen closet, vanity
Bsmnt				
Utility	7 x 8.5	Carpet	Paper	Closet, washer/dryer hookups
Ofc/Den	10 x 11	Carpet	Paper	Double closet

Lot: 1.37 acres   **Heating:** Gas   **Cooling:** Central air   **Water/Sewer:** Public

Agent: Jon Witner

Activity 5-6: Key Web Page Copy and Proofread in a Team

1 Open the data disk file *848321* and save it as *Act5-6si*.

2 Key the information from the owner's fact sheet below into the file.

3 Use team proofreading to check the Web page copy against the information below. Make sure to check the copy at the top of the page as well as the text you keyed.

4 Apply proofreaders' marks to any errors you find in the Web page copy.

5 Make any needed corrections, and turn in your final corrected copy.

Fact Sheet

- First bedroom is 19 x 14. Carpet, paper/paint. Ceiling fan, walk-in closet.
- Second bedroom—carpeted. 13.5 x 12. Painted, ceiling fan, double closet.
- Third bedroom—carpet. 11 x 13. Painted, ceiling fan, double closet.
- Foyer is papered, 18 x 14, with marble floors & coat closet.
- One bath has vinyl flooring, 11 x 5. Papered. Tub/shower, vanity, medicine cabinet.
- Other bath is 12 x 14, carpeted, paper/paint. Double vanity, linen closet, hot tub & shower.
- Living room is 17.5 x 11. Painted, carpeted.
- Kitchen is 22 x 14.5. Has vinyl floor, papered. Ceiling fan, island w/snack bar, pantry, storage.
- Dining room is 14 x 13.5. Carpeted, papered. Chandelier.
- Full basement (18.5 x 24.5). Finished family room. Carpeted, painted.
- Utility room upstairs: 7 x 8, with vinyl floor, painted walls, storage cabinets.
- Mudroom, 9.5 x 8. Painted walls, vinyl floor. Storage cabinets.

© GettyImages/PhotoDisc

→ 204 W. Elm St.—$279,900

→ 2-story, 3 BR, 2 BA

→ Formal LR, DR

→ Dbl. exposed stairway

→ Extra-large eat-in kitchen

→ Atrium, fenced-in backyard

→ 1-car detached garage

→ Central air, gas heat, public water, sewer

→ Lot size 86 x 120

Activity 5-7: **Proofread a Scanned Document in a Team**

The document below was scanned and imported into a word processing file. In the process, it lost much of its formatting. It also contains errors resulting from the scanning.

1 Open the data disk file *Voice Mail* and save it as *Act5-7si.*

2 Use team proofreading to check the file against the document below. One team member should proofread the file and apply proofreaders' marks to any errors. The other team member should then proofread the file a second time.

3 Make any needed corrections, and turn in your final corrected copy.

KITSTROM CORPORATION
VOICE MAIL GUIDELINES

YOU ARE THE COMPANY WHEN YOU ANSWER THE PHONE.

At Kitstrom Corporation, our policy is to use voice mail only when the office is closed or an employee is not available to take calls. Our employees do not use voice mail to screen calls.

Strive to make a good first and lasting impression. Remember that you are the company when you answer the phone. Tone is very important. Smile when you record your message.

The first few times you record a voice mail message, try calling from another phone and listening to your message. Does it give clients the information they need? Does it have a warm, professional tone?

Recording Voice Mail Messages

- Keep your message short.

- Use a warm, professional tone.

- Speak slowly and clearly.

- Update your message frequently. If you will be on vacation or out of town for several days, be sure your message includes that information.

- Always include instructions on how to reach the operator or another member of your team in case callers need immediate assistance.

- Ask callers to leave their name, phone number, and a brief message.

- Check your messages often, and return calls promptly.

Use the Grammar Checker

FOCUS

Does the following text contain errors in grammar or style? Circle *Yes* or *No* for each item.

> The problem was solved by some of the students.   Yes   No

> This editing job complete on time.   Yes   No

> All activities may not be assigned to all students.   Yes   No

Grammar Checker Features

A skillful proofreader will use every available tool to find and correct all types of errors in a document. Errors in grammar can be difficult to detect, more so than errors in keying and spelling. You can use your software's grammar checker to check a document or selected text for grammar and style errors.

The grammar checker can be set to check for errors in two ways: automatically as you key or all at once when you select the grammar-check option. Either way, the process is nearly the same. The feature marks text that may contain an error. If the feature is checking as you key, you can right-click the marked text for a pop-up menu that suggests changes or explains the error. If you are running a check all at once, the suggested changes or explanation appears in a dialog box.

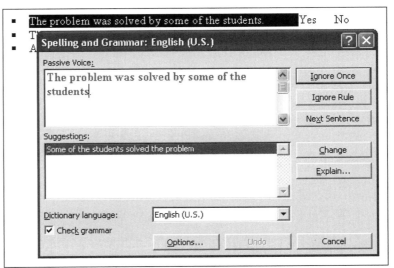

The Microsoft® Word Spelling and Grammar dialog box

Dialog boxes offer various options to help you in correcting text. Pop-up menus have some of these options, too. The options and their exact names vary, but they generally include the following:

Option	Result
Ignore or Ignore Once	The grammar checker ignores the error and moves to the next item.
Ignore All or Ignore Rule	The grammar checker ignores that error or type of error throughout the document.
Next Sentence	You fix the error, and the grammar checker moves to the next error.
Change	The grammar checker lets you choose a suggested edit or change the text yourself.
Change All	The grammar checker makes the correction throughout the document.
Resume	The grammar checker starts checking again after you have finished editing an item in the document.
Delete	If the same word appears twice in a row (*dog is is coming*), the grammar checker deletes the extra word.
Explain	The grammar checker explains the grammar or style rule.
Undo	The grammar checker reverses the last correction that was made. If clicked again, it will reverse the correction before that, and so on.

In Microsoft® Word, the grammar checker is usually run together with the spelling checker, and it works in a similar way. Just as the spelling checker compares words in a document to its built-in dictionary, the grammar checker compares text to a set of grammar and style rules that have been programmed into the software. If a rule has not been programmed into the software, the grammar checker will not find errors based on that rule.

Limits of Grammar Checkers

Grammar checkers do not detect all grammar and style errors. In the second example in the Focus activity, *This editing job complete on time*, the Microsoft® Word grammar checker failed to detect that this was an incomplete sentence. In addition, grammar checkers sometimes propose changes that are incorrect. For example, Microsoft® Word 97 suggested changing the sentence to *These editing jobs complete on time* or *This editing job complete on time*. A third problem with grammar checkers is that they sometimes find "errors" that are actually correct. When you use a grammar checker, you should look carefully at each error it detects to ensure it is an error.

Use the grammar checker as you do the spelling checker. Run it after you have finished writing a document, before you proofread it. As you proofread, be alert for grammar and style errors that the grammar checker may have missed. If you make a lot of changes to a document, run the grammar checker again.

A style manual and an English grammar text can be helpful for proofreading. Libraries and the Internet offer many resources for checking grammar. Online resources include style manuals and grammar services where you can pose a question. Some services charge and some are free. If you need to jog your memory on grammar rules for this or any other lesson's activities, you can consult the *Grammar* file in the Reference Guide folder on your student data disk.

Activity 6-1: Proofread for Run-Ons and Sentence Fragments

On each blank line, write *S* for *complete sentence*, *R* for *run-on sentence*, or *F* for *sentence fragment*. Use proofreaders' marks to correct run-on sentences and fragments.

Examples

___S___ Are you going to try out for show choir this year?

___F___ After we drove through the Badlands National Park. ∧ we ate lunch

___ 1 Prairie dogs live in towns that may include thousands of individuals.

___ 2 One prairie dog stands guard while the others look for food, the sentry gives a warning bark if it senses danger.

___ 3 This afternoon at 4 p.m. when we get off work.

___ 4 We plan to travel together to the state computer conference next month.

___ 5 The purple martins arriving in our city in March an early sign of spring.

Activity 6-2: Proofread for Parallel Sentence Parts

Write *P* for each sentence that is parallel in structure. Write *X* for each sentence that is not. Use proofreaders' marks to correct sentences that are not parallel.

Examples

___X___ He got the job by working hard and ~~because he follows~~ directions well.

___P___ We all need encouragement and recognition.

___ 1 Susan wanted to take a vacation and to visit old friends.

___ 2 He likes to play soccer and cooking on a charcoal grill.

___ 3 Meg goes to school in the morning and works in the afternoon.

___ 4 She had to choose between walking to work and the bus.

___ 5 Mr. Melton received the promotion because he is a good team player and for being an effective supervisor.

Activity 6-3: Proofread for Subject-Verb Agreement

The following sentences contain correct and incorrect verb forms. If the verb is correct, draw a single line under the subject and a double line under the verb. Use proofreaders' marks to correct any incorrect verbs.

Examples

Each of my classes are 50 minutes long. *is*

Several of her friends are my friends also.

1 Neither David nor Peggy is attending the meeting.

2 She and her husband is involved in several community civic projects.

3 The professors at the university treats all students with proper respect.

4 The honors banquet at the College of Business each year is a black-tie affair.

5 Their request for new textbooks have been approved.

Activity 6-4: Proofread for Pronoun Case

Draw a double line under the correct pronoun of the two in parentheses.

Examples

May Shala and (**me, I**) sit together in the front row?

Mr. Rodriguez said, "(**She**, **Her**) and (**me, I**) were the last ones to leave the luncheon."

1 The swim coach asked Jacob and (**me, I**) to work with the younger swimmers.

2 Let's split the cost of the pizza between Joanne and (**me, I**).

3 (**Us, We**) students raised $4,000 for the American Cancer Society.

4 Was it (**she, her**) who admitted to plagiarizing the article that appeared on the Internet?

5 (**Him, He**) and I are making plans to attend the Olympics this summer.

Activity 6-5: Proofread for Plurals

Write the correct plural form of the underlined noun or pronoun. Write *C* if the underlined noun or pronoun is correct.

Examples

_____babies_____	The <u>baby</u> were all crying at the same time in the nursery.
_____C_____	We like to watch the <u>fish</u> swimming around in our patio pond.

_____ 1 The truth is, one must stand on one's own two <u>foot</u>.

_____ 2 In our travels, we saw many beautiful <u>deer</u> idly grazing.

_____ 3 Does the recipe call for one or two <u>tomato</u>?

_____ 4 My grandmother has many <u>hobby</u>; her favorite is gardening.

_____ 5 I hardly can wait until the <u>fig</u> are ripe.

Activity 6-6: Proofread for Possessives

Draw a double line under the correct possessive form of the noun or pronoun in parentheses.

Examples

My (**<u>mom's</u>**, **moms'**) wedding dress still fits her perfectly.

All of the (**boy's**, **<u>boys'</u>**) lockers need to be replaced.

1 Ms. (**Jones'**, **Jones's**) presentation covered the important points.

2 Each (**night's**, **nights'**) performance had (**its**, **it's**) own special theme.

3 The six seniors failed to ask their (**parent's**, **parents'**) permission to stay longer.

4 I sent (**hers**, **her's**) yesterday by express mail.

5 The (**children's**, **childrens'**) summer program starts tomorrow.

Activity 6-7: Proofread Sentences for Grammar and Style Errors

Each of the following sentences contains one grammar or style error. Find the error and use proofreaders' marks to correct it.

Examples

Several couple stayed for hours listening to the bluegrass music.

While we waited for the next train. ∧ we talked about the trip.

1 Is *White Fang* a story about wolfs or merely wild dogs?

2 Either Yu-Lan or Ginny are ready to be promoted.

3 The new shipment of computer software.

4 Each doctors' office hours were posted on her door.

5 Every girl brought their money for the field trip.

6 How many countrys are represented in the United Nations?

7 Sunita controls her weight by eating three good meals and 30 minutes of exercise each day.

8 The movies listed in the newspaper starts tomorrow.

9 Juan and me will take a later flight.

10 We worked until 9 o'clock, then we headed home.

11 The Smith's house went up for sale last week.

12 He is going both to Los Angeles and San Diego.

13 The mens' football league plays every Saturday afternoon.

14 All students have to take a sport in the fall, in the winter months, and in the springtime.

Activity 6-8: Check Grammar in a Memo

Proofread the following memo for grammar and style errors. Use proofreaders' marks to mark corrections.

TO: <student mail merge>

FROM: Peter Coleman, Principal

DATE: October 23, 200-

SUBJECT: Peer Mediation

Several weeks ago, we conducted a survey on peer mediation. A process in which trained student moderators work with students to help them settle disputes in a positive way. Many of you thought that peer mediation might work good at our school. As a result, we will start a peer mediation program in late November.

Disputes in areas such as friendship issues, teasing, and bullying will be referred by teachers or school administrators for mediation. The mediator will act as a neutral third party. Peer mediation don't focus on assigning blame. Mediators ask questions and encourage each person to tell their story. In this way, they help students find a way to settle the problem and get along.

Several of you have expressed a interest in being a peer mediator. The Counseling Center will conduct a training workshop for them students on November 8 and 9. Mr. Juan Martinez and Mrs. Erin Collins will work closely with you and will teach you how to approach the task of mediating. Mrs. Collins daughter, Candy, will assist as an intern.

If you are interest in being a peer mediator, please stop by the Counseling Center to register. The trainers and myself look forward to working with you.

Activity 6-9: **Proofread a Report**

1 Open the data disk file *After School, Then What* and save it as *Act6-9si*.

2 Run the grammar checker, making corrections as needed. Follow these guidelines in making corrections:

   ✔ Do not correct uses of the passive voice.

   ✔ Watch out for "errors" the grammar checker finds that are actually correct.

3 Proofread the document. Watch for errors that your grammar checker may have missed.

4 Make any needed corrections, and turn in your final corrected copy.

Activity 6-10: **Check Grammar in an Intranet Posting**

1 Open the data disk file *Teamwork* and save it as *Act6-10si*.

2 Run the grammar checker, making corrections as needed. Watch out for corrections the grammar checker suggests that are not correct.

3 Proofread the document. Watch for errors that your grammar checker may have missed. **Bonus:** Make two changes for parallelism.

4 Make any needed corrections, and turn in your final corrected copy.

Activity 6-11: **Check Grammar in a Report**

1 Open the data disk file *Australia* and save it as *Act6-11si*. Though this document is single-spaced on the next page, your data disk file is correctly formatted as a report, with double spacing.

2 Make the corrections indicated in the marked-up copy on page 49.

3 Run the grammar checker, making corrections as needed. Do not correct uses of the passive voice.

4 Proofread the document. Watch for errors that your grammar checker may have missed.

5 Make any needed corrections, and turn in your final corrected copy.

A GLIMPSE "DOWN UNDER"

Australia is a island continent similar in size to the United States excluding Alaska and Hawaii. It is known as the land down under because it is in the Southern Hemisphere. Australia appears on a world globe as a land below the other continents, although there are other countrys in the Southern Hemisphere.

General Information

  The population of Australia lives mostly along it's coastlines. Since Australia has considerably less people than the United States, this leaves Central Australia very sparsely populated. Much of this area consist of cattle stations, ranches about the same size as them found in the southwestern United States. Children who live in the remote outback have access to education through the School of the Air, a radio and correspondence school located in Alice Springs.

  Australia's seasons are roughly the same as those in the United States; however, they occur at exact opposite times of the year. Australia's summer is during our winter.

Diverse Animal Life

  The koala bear is actually not a bear at all, it is a marsupial. The koala lives in eucalyptus trees and fed upon the leaves. Though several hundred types of eucalyptus trees exist in the forests of Australia, the koala feeds only on certain types. Eucalyptus leaves are nutritious to koalas but toxic to humans. The sap has a relaxing effect that encourages sleep, which may explain why koalas sleep about 18 hours a day!

  Animal life in Australia is quite different from that in many other places in the world. The emu is a flightless bird native to Australia and is larger than any bird native to the United States. Many of Australia's mammals are marsupials, which means the female has a pocket or pouch to carry her young. One example of an Australian marsupial is the kangaroo. A characteristic unique to emus and kangaroos is that neither can move backward due to its leg structure!

  The Great Barrier Reef lays off the northeastern coast of Australia. The numerous coral structures of the reef forms a habitat for a considerable variety of sea life. On a clear day, a ride in a boat with glass windows at the bottom provides an excellent below-the-waterline view of these structures and the many beautifully colored fish.

The Aborigines

  The native people of Australia are the aborigines. The aborigines' way of life was completely separate from that of European settlers. The aboriginal lifestyle is rich in culture and tradition. Ayers Rock is a sacred site of the aborigine people and is the larger single rock known in the world. At sunset, the rock seems to change color progressively though varying hues of red and orange. A beautiful sight.

Conclusion

This glimpse of Australia only briefly portrays the diversity and beauty of this continent. Visitors with every kind of interest will find something in the land down under to do and remember.

Activity 6-12: Get Grammar and Style Help Online

1 Online writing labs, or *OWLs*, help people improve their writing skills. Go to a search engine such as Google (http://www.google.com) and search for an online writing lab.

2 Explore several of the online labs you find. Bookmark one that offers useful help on grammar. Write the URL here:

_____

3 Write a summary of one grammar rule or tip you did not know before that you learned from this site.

_____

_____

4 Stylebooks offer sets of rules for grammar, punctuation, and style. *The Elements of Style* by William Strunk, Jr., is a good stylebook. Access an online copy of this stylebook at http://www.bartleby.com/141/.

    a Click rule 7 under "Elementary Rules of Usage." After reading about this rule, use proofreaders' marks to correct the following sentence.

    Riding my bicycle, the dog chased me all the way to Front Street.

    b Read about rules 11–13 under "Elementary Principles of Composition." Then revise the following sentences so that they follow the three rules.

    These are the four steps that should be followed by every employee at our store.

    _____

    Annie did not remember to lock the door.

    _____

    In spite of the fact that he was tired, Dave stayed to help.

    _____

5 Search the Internet for another grammar Web site that you find useful. You can search for a general site or a site that covers a particular rule, such as subject-verb agreement. Write the URL here.

_____

Make the Punctuation Check

FOCUS

How would you punctuate these sentences?

> Joseph Collignan said Punctuation is the sound of your voice on paper.

> According to Johann Wolfgang von Goethe When ideas fail words come in very handy.

> J K Rowling wrote It is our choices . . . that show what we truly are far more than our abilities.

Punctuate for Clarity

Every well-written document relies on punctuation to convey the writer's message effectively and clearly. Punctuation is vital to getting your point across to your readers. A correctly punctuated document will read well, will flow from one thought to the next, and will deliver the message that the writer intended. Good writers today tend to punctuate sensibly and less.

The following marks are used by proofreaders to correct errors in punctuation:

PROOFREADERS MARKS FOR PUNCTUATION	
Insert period.	at the end⊙
Insert comma.	next week‸
Insert quotation marks.	⌄The Road Not Taken⌄
Insert apostrophe.	couldn⌄t
Insert other marks.	Did you do it‽

Seven Common Errors in Punctuation

Nearly everyone makes errors in punctuation sometimes. Seven common punctuation errors are listed on the next page. Do any of them give you problems? Can you think of others that might? How would you correct these examples?

1. Using a comma between two independent clauses without using a conjunction

   Incorrect: The two girls went to the mall, they shopped for new bathing suits and beach towels.

2. Failing to use a comma after phrases or dependent clauses at the beginning of a sentence

   Incorrect: Because they did not study for the test the students received poor grades.

3. Failing to use commas to set off phrases and clauses that are nonessential, or not needed to complete the meaning of the sentence

   Incorrect: The Akashi Kaikyo Bridge which extends 12,828 feet is the longest suspension bridge in the world.

4. Using a comma to separate two predicates (verbs and their related words) that have the same subject

   Incorrect: Her son is quite good at playing soccer, and enjoys volleyball.

5. Failing to use apostrophes in possessives

   Incorrect: My friends company donates thousands of dollars worth of food and clothing to homeless shelters each year.

6. Using apostrophes in plurals

   Incorrect: At 5:30 a.m., the children and their fathers' are driving to Atlanta to attend a Brave's baseball game.

7. Writing *it's* or *its'* to form the possessive of *it*.

   Incorrect: Atlanta is known for it's Southern hospitality.

Grammar checkers can be useful in detecting punctuation errors. However, they do not always detect every mistake in punctuation. In addition, grammar checkers sometimes find "errors" that are not errors or suggest incorrect changes.

When you are proofreading a word-processed file, use a grammar checker first and then proofread. Do not rely on the grammar checker to find every punctuation error.

Aids to Punctuation

A grammar handbook or style manual can be useful for checking punctuation. Libraries offer many resources, as does the Internet. These include online style manuals, online writing labs (OWLs), college and university Web sites, and sites maintained by editors and other experts. Often, just keying your question in a search engine will yield a list of Web sites where you can find the answer.

To jog your memory on punctuation rules, consult the *Punctuation* file in the Reference Guide folder on your student data disk. The *Glossary* file, located in the same folder, provides definitions of grammar terms.

Activity 7-1: **Proofread for Commas and End Punctuation**

Proofread the following sentences. Use proofreaders' marks to insert commas, periods, and question marks as needed and take out incorrect commas. Circle the one correctly punctuated sentence.

1 Because of deer rabbits armadillos, and too much rain our garden is ruined.

2 Our Chinese friends are eager to try American foods see American cities and visit American homes but they also want to share their culture with us

3 Have you learned how to play the violin or have you given up learning to play it

4 Mary, my next-door neighbor, gave me roses, daylilies, and irises for my garden.

5 The Carolina Wren, that I rescued, is ready to fly

6 The Cub Scouts deciding not to explore any further that day returned to camp

Activity 7-2: **Proofread for Colons and Semicolons**

Proofread the following sentences. Use proofreaders' marks to insert colons and semicolons as needed and take them out if they are incorrect. Circle the one correctly punctuated sentence.

1 I can hardly wait until 5;00, when we leave on a two-week trek over rugged mountain trails to our favorite camp.

2 The sun is out today; however, it has rained on and off for the last 14 days.

3 If you hurry, you can get to the post office in time the last delivery goes out at 5 p.m.

4 The delicious pound cake contains four different flavors vanilla, butter, coconut, and almond.

5 Last summer we visited: San Francisco, California, Salem, Oregon, and Seattle, Washington.

6 Andrew was a Category 5 hurricane its wind speeds reached 165 miles per hour.

Activity 7-3: Proofread for Apostrophes and Quotation Marks

Proofread the following sentences. Use proofreaders' marks to insert apostrophes and quotation marks as needed and take them out if they are incorrect. Circle the one correctly punctuated sentence.

1 Tomorrows lunchtime seminar, Handling Stress on the Job, will take place from noon to 1 p.m. in the cafeteria.

2 My friend's husband walks 4 miles a day.

3 An ant can lift 20 times it's own body weight.

4 Henry David Thoreau said, Success usually comes to those who are too busy to be looking for it.

5 Due to drought in the Midwest, where my cousins' live, fire is a constant threat.

6 June asked, 'Do you know where I might find recipe's for zucchini and tomato relishes?'

Activity 7-4: Proofread for All Punctuation Marks

Proofread the following sentences. Use proofreaders' marks to insert punctuation marks as needed and take them out if they are incorrect. Circle the one correctly punctuated sentence.

1 With DSL, you can be on the Internet, and still get phone calls.

2 She said Are you planning to stay in Washington

3 The slow leak technology used in todays tires allows ample time to reach a repair shop before a tire goes flat providing a blowout doesnt occur first

4 A successful fishing trip requires these items good weather proper bait and tackle a good fishing spot and a stringer of fish.

5 Ms. Holmes favorite books include *"The Lord of the Rings"* *"Around the World in 80 Days"* and *"A Christmas Carol"*.

6 Delaware's border with Maryland runs through two towns: Marydel and Delmar.

Activity 7-5: **Check Paragraphs for Punctuation Errors**

Proofread the following paragraphs. Use proofreaders' marks to insert punctuation marks as needed and take them out if they are incorrect.

Just how important is exercise? Well this question might be phrased more appropriately How important is good health.

A recent government study showed that 31 percent of adults in the United States are obese. Obesity means weighing more than 30 percent of ones ideal body weight; and it can have serious effects on peoples health. Obesity can increase the risk of heart disease; hypertension; stroke; depression; and many other health problems.

Exercise that strengthens heart muscle is known as cardiovascular exercise Cardiovascular exercise includes any activity that raises the heart rate for an extended period of time. The following are examples of cardiovascular activities walking jogging hiking biking swimming and skiing. Activities like these help people lose weight, and lessen their risk of developing many diseases. The U.S. Surgeon General recommends that people get at least 30 minutes worth of moderate exercise most days of the week.

Activity 7-6: **Apply Six Basic Punctuation Rules**

INTERNET

1 Visit the Web site of the Writing Across the Curriculum program at Northern Illinois University at http://www.engl.niu.edu/wac/punctrls.html. Read the Six Basic Punctuation Rules listed on this page.

2 Using word processing software, compose two sentences for each of the six rules. If you need help with a rule, click the "Get more explanation" link.

3 Save your file as *Act7-6si*.

Activity 7-7: Proofread an E-Mail for Punctuation Errors

1 You and a friend have agreed to proofread each other's Internet research assignments before e-mailing them to your language arts teacher. Your friend's e-mail is the data disk file *Internet Research Assignment*. Open this file and save it as *Act7-7si*.

2 Proofread your friend's e-mail. Make any needed corrections, and turn in your final corrected copy.

Activity 7-8: Proofread a Letter for Punctuation Errors

1 Open the data disk file *Team Parent* and save it as *Act7-8si*.

2 Proofread the letter. Make any needed corrections, and turn in your final corrected copy.

Activity 7-9: Proofread a Memo for Punctuation Errors

1 Open the data disk file *Digital Time Stamp* and save it as *Act7-9si*.

2 Make the changes marked in the copy of the memo on page 57.

3 Proofread the memo for punctuation and keyboarding errors. Make any needed corrections, and turn in your final corrected copy.

TO: Board Members

FROM: Danielle Storms, Research Strategist

DATE: October 21, 200-

SUBJECT: November Board Meeting Agenda Item

~~While searching on the Internet~~ recently I ~~discovered~~ *learned about* a new ~~idea in~~ technology that might help cut costs and imporve efficiency for our company. ~~Please take the time to famliarize yourself with it before the November board meeting on Thursday, November 17.~~

Our clients rely on our closing books on precise dates to meet their committments to their own clients and ~~to~~ to tax authorities. We can streamline our procedure for verifying dates by using a digital time-stamping service, or DTS. A DTS issues electronic time stamps that that certify the date and time a document was created, or last modified. A time-stamped document cannot be changed without ~~detectom.~~ *detection.* Digital time stamps are legally binding

Digital time stamping guarantees a savings of both time and money. It is also a very reliable and secure ~~way to verify dates and times for a document.~~ When you select a file to be time-stamped your computer sends a (the DTS) special unique number, or fingerprint, based on the files contents. The DTS puts the number, a long with the date and time it was received into a coded electronic envelope. It then sends our computer a digital time-stamp certificate. The document never leaves our computer system. The DTS cannot read the document, therefore the content is secure.

Please ~~take the time to~~ review the attached information about digital time stamping. ~~As you persue the information please~~ jot down any questions or ~~ideas~~ *comments, pro or con, and* to discuss at the board meeting. Just a reminder ~~but~~ we meet this month on Thursday November 17, at 230 pm.

Attachments

c   Ethan T. Kyle, Chairperson
       Melissa K. El-Kharmia
       Whitney S. Ussery
       Jordan T. Browne
       Erin E. Coleman

Alphabitize by last name to follow chairperson.

Activity 7-10: Proofread a Report for Punctuation Errors

Proofread the first page of a report, applying proofreaders' marks to any punctuation and keyboarding errors.

IT'S MY FUTURE: WHAT AM I GOING TO DO WITH IT?

My interest is in the future because I am
going to spend the rest of my life there.
—Charles F. Kettering

A topic frequently discussed on secondary school campuses is what students plan to do after graduation? Many students who plan to go to college havent the slightest idea about what field of study to pursue or what job would be suitable given their interests, skills, abilities, and personality. Students who can not or do not plan to go to college, often do not have career plans either.

Schools offer many resources for people in this predicament. Career plannning services such as the student advising center and career center provide personality and interest inventory testing; information about various career options, and an up-to-date list of jobs projected to be the most needed in the future. Through campus services students can find mentors. They can also explore different careers through job shadowing, internships, and similar opportunities.

The Internet provides a wealth of resources and informaiton. For example, the Web site http://www.myfuture.com, thought aimed at students considering a military career offers information and insights on other career-related topics. At this site, students can learn about volunteer and internship opportunities, technical and vocational schools, and apprenticeships. The Web site http://jobstar.org offers career guides information on finding jobs in the hidden job market and tips on resumes.

Proofread for Mechanical Errors

The following paragraph contains seven mechanical errors. Can you find them all? Circle each error you discover.

> We have received eleven applications for the position of occupational health advisor. our personnel director has reviewed them and has checked references. May i meet with you on Tues., december first, at ten a.m. to choose the applicants we will interview?

The Mechanics of Writing

Mechanical errors are mistakes specific to writing.

Errors in grammar or style are usually errors whether we make them in writing or speech. For example, the sentence *Her and him walked home* contains an error. It does not matter whether you write the sentence or say it. The error is still there. An error in capitalization, on the other hand, is an error in writing alone. If you write the sentence *i walked home*, it contains an error. If you say the sentence, however, it does not.

Different writers and instructors include different errors in those they consider mechanical. For example, some people think of errors in punctuation as mechanical errors. Some include errors in formatting documents. Punctuation and document formatting are covered in Lessons 7 and 10. In this lesson, the following types of mechanical errors are covered:

> Capitalization
> Abbreviations
> Bold and italics
> Writing numbers

Like rules for grammar, spelling, and style, the mechanics of good writing promote clarity. Following a widely accepted set of rules makes your writing easier to read and understand.

Mechanical errors occur often.

Signs Change; Trends Change

Road signs change as improvements occur along a highway. Rules change to allow for improvements in writing. Rules in capitalization, number usage, abbreviations, and other mechanics change when a need for improvement is evident. Changes in society, technology, and business prompt changes in the mechanics of writing. Several recent trends in writing are described below.

> **Capitalize less.** Most business titles, such as *chief executive officer*, are capitalized only when they come before a person's name, not when they follow it or stand alone. The names of offices or committees usually are not capitalized unless you are writing for a specific organization that prefers to capitalize them.

> **Use figures instead of words with measurements, weights, and dimensions.** In the past, figures were usually used only in technical writing. Readers today value their time. They want to be able to read and understand a document as quickly as possible. Figures are often easier to understand than words.

> **Avoid abbreviations in material intended for a general audience.** The exception is common abbreviations like *Mrs.*, *Mr.*, or *Dr.* If you are not sure your audience will understand an abbreviation, spell it out.

> **Avoid using italics to emphasize words.** Write in a way that gives your ideas the emphasis they need.

Aids for Finding Mechanical Errors

Spelling and grammar checkers will detect some common mechanical errors. They will not detect all mechanical errors, however, and they sometimes find "errors" that are actually correct. Do not rely on a spelling or grammar checker to find all mechanical errors in a document. Run both checkers first. Then proofread to catch any errors they missed.

An English textbook or stylebook is good to have on hand for checking mechanics. Libraries often keep copies of several stylebooks in their reference section, so they are available to users. Internet resources include Web sites maintained by editors and other experts, college and university Web sites, electronic style manuals, and online writing labs (OWLs). Often, you can get the answer for your question by keying it in a search engine. For help with mechanics, you can consult the *Mechanics* file in the Reference Guide folder of your student data disk.

Activity 8-1: Find Capitalization and Italics Errors

Use proofreaders' marks to identify capitalization and italics errors in the following sentences. Circle the one correct sentence.

1 Did you know that the louisiana territory was purchased from france in 1803 for $15 million?

2 Fewer students enroll in calculus I, II, and III.

3 The national weather service, which is part of noaa, issues more than 15,000 severe storm and tornado watches and warnings each year.

4 Did you enjoy your trip to Asia as much as your trip to the Australian Outback?

5 The former department head, dr. a. w. kohler, is now a Professor Emeritus.

6 In 1917, jeannette rankin became the first woman to serve in the house of representatives.

7 Several members are of south korean, thai, and filipino descent.

8 Hurricane georges caused a considerable amount of rain in the southeast.

9 Then i asked, "have you read 'the divine comedy' by dante alighieri?"

10 Last year, we invited chinese friends to celebrate thanksgiving day with us, and they invited us to celebrate the moon festival with their family and friends.

11 the treaty of versailles, which ended world war I, was signed on june 28, 1919.

12 During our visit to new york, we lunched at times square and attended the plays "thoroughly modern millie" and "oklahoma."

13 We hiked North for two days on the appalachian trail.

14 He was stationed at the white house from 1953 to 1961.

Activity 8-2: **Find Abbreviation, Italics, and Number Errors**

Use proofreaders' marks to identify errors in abbreviations, italics, and number use.
Circle the one correct sentence.

1   After her children were grown, my mother returned to college and earned
    her bs and ms degrees in education and technology, respectively.

2   Her husband had his Ph.D. in education and taught for 32 years at his
    alma mater, Loyola University.

3   Mike Powell holds the world long jump record of twenty-nine ft four in.

4   The vice pres., 2 other officers, and thirteen members-at-large attended the
    regional technology convention in Omaha, Neb.

5   Doctor D. Wade Locke said that sixty-two percent of teens don't get enough
    exercise.

6   The tour will begin at nine-thirty AM on Oct. 7th at the Empire State Bldg.

7   I saved five hundred dollars by building my own computer.

8   We have eight and a half cartons of three-point-five-inch disks in stock; 3/4
    of our orders now are for CDs.

9   The abbreviation etc means "and so forth," the abbreviation eg means "for
    example," and the abbreviation ie means "that is."

10 N.Y. is the only city where the majority of workers—55%—use public trans-
    portation to get to work.

11 13 young people in our city worked this summer with Habitat for Humanity
    and helped to build 7 houses.

12 He counted twenty-seven birds on one power line and nine on another.

13 Last week, they ordered 12 25-pound boxes of grapes.

Activity 8-3: Proofread a Resume

Proofread the following resume for errors in capitalization, abbreviations, italics, and numbers. Use proofreaders' marks to mark corrections.

GEORGIANNA CHRISTINE DINERSTEIN

2901 Chestnut Street
Shreveport, LA 71109-2215
(318) 555-0167

CAREER OBJECTIVE
To teach business and office subjects and related technology at the community college or vocational-technical level.

EDUCATION
ms. Business Education and Technology, Beall State Univ., Alexandria, Louisiana. May 2005. Served as teaching graduate assistant and treasurer of Delta Pi Epsilon.

bs. Technology Teacher Education, Beall State Univ., Alexandria, Louisiana. May 2004. graduated magna cum laude. Served as president of Pi Omega Pi. Member of Kappa Delta Pi.

SPECIAL SKILLS
Environments: Microsoft® Windows® XP
Application software: Corel® WordPerfect® 8, Adobe®
                      PageMaker® 6.5, Microsoft® Office XP,
                      Microsoft® Works

EXPERIENCE
First Trust Bank, Shreveport, Louisiana. Administrative asst., 1998-2000.
- Keyed, filed, & updated loan documents.
- Installed new filing system.
- Paid & filed bills.
- Answered phone & dispatched personnel.

County Day Care, Shreveport, Louisiana. Instructor, 1998-2000.
- Taught 4- & 5-year-old children keyboarding skills.
- Instructed caregivers on use of keyboarding software.

REFERENCES
Request portfolio from beall state university placement office, p.o box 104, Alexandria, LA 71309-0104, (318) 555-0132.

Activity 8-4: **Proofread a Flyer**

1 Open the data disk file *Day Out* and save it as *Act8-4si*.

2 Locate the star in the document. Click the star and hold the left mouse button to drag it to the top of the tree.

3 Proofread the flyer for errors in capitalization, abbreviations, and numbers. Make any needed corrections, and turn in your final corrected copy.

Activity 8-5: **Proofread an Intranet Posting**

1 Open the data disk file *Job Shadow* and save it as *Act8-5si*.

2 Proofread the document for errors in capitalization, abbreviations, and numbers. Make any needed corrections, and turn in your final corrected copy.

Activity 8-6: **Proofread a Letter**

1 Open the data disk file *CCS Job Letter* and save it as *Act8-6si*.

2 Proofread the letter for errors in capitalization, abbreviations, numbers, and keyboarding. Make any needed corrections, and turn in your final corrected copy.

Activity 8-7: **Proofread a News Release**

1 Open the data disk file *Mentoring Seminar* and save it as *Act8-7si*. Although the document is single-spaced on the next page, your data disk file is correctly formatted as a news release, with double spacing.

2 Make the corrections indicated in the marked-up copy on page 65.

3 Proofread the news release for errors in capitalization, abbreviations, italics, numbers, and keyboarding.

4 Exchange papers with a teammate. Proofread each other's work, marking any errors with proofreaders' marks. Write your name as proofreader on your teammate's document.

5 Turn in the final corrected document and the draft your teammate proofread.

METRO GLOBAL COMMODITIES
1002 Brett Favre Pass
Green Bay, WI 54304-3736
(920) 555-0100   **(920) 555-0102 FAX**

News Release   **Contact:** Jessica a Thurman
                                                      For release: immediately

GREEN BAY, Wi September 22nd, 200-. In cooperation with Kessler Univ., Metro Global Commodities (MCG) recently announced its annual professional seminar, "mentoring for a brighter future." The seminar will be held each Saturday in Feb. from 1000 am to two pm on-site at MGC's corporate headquarters. MGC personnel will offer mentoring in the following areas: cost analysis, manufacturing efficiency, advertising and sales, packaging and shipping, warehousing, product distribution, profit analysis, personnel, market analysis, and personnel evaluation.

In the april 200- issue of **Business Management**, MGC published a recent study of challenges that may companies face. The study revealed one major problem: a critical shortage of experienced employees. It also identified 4 key factors that contribute to employer shortages: one—an increase in the no. of college-bound students, two—downsizing and three—redistribution in the work force, and four—early retirment. The study over whelmingly indicated that as the workplace rapidly changes, jobs once considered routine are becoming more complex. In addition, new jobs demand more specialized levels of education training and skills. The study noted, "downsized companies must do more and more with less and less. corporate management recognizes the need to identify and pass on the accumulated knowledge and skills of employees who have reached or are nearing retirement age." The study reported that seventy-five percent of managers surveyed voiced this concern but said they did not now how to secure this knowledge.

Careful investigation into what has worked solutions in other areas has revealed that mentoring is the one way to promote ongoing retain corporate knowledge. It is a win-win situation for all concerned. Mentoring is a process by which trained and skilled employers help to train new employees, who in turn train future employees.

College student who are interested in a manufacturing and marketing enterprise will benefit from the valuable hands-on experience this seminar will offers. Students who complete the seminar will receive 2 semester hrs. of college credit. Metro Global Commodities also guarantees summer and holiday employment to students who complete the seminar training as well as preferential consideration fro full employment upon graduation. Registration is free. Interested students must reregister by January 10th. To register, students can call Ms Jessica A. Thurman at 555-0106.

###

Activity 8-8: Proofread a Tri-Fold Brochure

This document is one side of a tri-fold brochure. Proofread it for errors in capitalization, abbreviations, italics, numbers, and keyboarding. Use proofreaders' marks to mark corrections.

FAYETTE RAFTING
WHITEWATER RAFTING

America's Favorite Water Sport

RIVER THRILLS
ADVENTURE VACATIONS
SCENIC CHALLENGES

APRIL THROUGH OCTOBER

To plan your trip, ask questions, or make your reservation, please e-mail or call the toll-free number below.

raftingexperts@fayetterafting.com
1-800-555-0100

ADVENTURE—rafting is one of many special pleasures available in the outdoors. May be you see yourself floating down a lazy river, enjoying nature at its best. Or maybe you'd like to be tossing and turning along a swiftly churning, thundrous river, anticipating white water or rapids around the next bend.

Either way, has you paddle along, you can admire the beautiful scenery—white foam, caves, colorful flora and fauna, & the raw power of the river or stream.

ACCESSIBILITY—Whatever your age and ability level, there's a **Fayette Rafting** adventure that's right for you. Rafting is a great way to work as a team, either with a group of friends or with total strangres.

Gauley river and new river provide some of the finest whitewater rafting in the country. Our team has twenty years' experience, and we're rated best for 200- by "Whitewater Adventures" magazine.

AVAILABILITY—Rafting is a seasonal sport. to provide maximum whitewater enjoyment, we schedule our rafting season form April through October.

Trips are available in varying lengths: 1/2-day, full-day, overnight, and up to to 6-day excursions.

ACCOMMODATIONS—**Fayette Rafting** trips generally require reservations at least a week in advance. Our fourteen-ft. rafts are self-bailing and hold 7 people. For overnight and multi-day trips, we offer meals grilled over a campfire be our tour guides. Lunches and dinners include fish, poultry, or beef or a vegetarian alternative. Drinks and snacks are are the responsibility of each individual.

Fayette Rafting provides life preservers and floatation devices & requires their use.

Call today to begin making planes for a **Fayette Rafting** trip, 1 you will never forget—never in your wildest dreams!

Proofread for Consistency

A poor idea well written is more likely to be accepted than a good idea poorly written.

—Isaac Asimov

The Value of Consistency

Checking a document for consistency is one of the most important tasks of proofreading. **Consistency** means that certain things are done the same way throughout a document. Documents should be consistent in style or tone, verb tense, punctuation, mechanics, formatting, and facts.

Consistency gives an impression of care and attention to detail that reflects well on writers and their organizations. In contrast, lack of consistency gives an impression of carelessness and inattention to detail. It also makes documents harder to read and understand.

Organizations think consistency is important. Many have their own style lists, model documents, or style manuals for employees to refer to when writing. Style manuals discuss topics such as how to format letters, memos, and reports, as well as how to ensure documents do not contain biased language.

Consistency Checks

Consider the following areas in which you can check your document for consistency.

Style or Tone. A document should be consistent in style or tone. For example, a sales letter written in general language should not suddenly switch to technical language. Documents should be made consistent in style and tone during writing and editing. The proofreader may sometimes have to make a correction.

Verb Tense, Punctuation, and Mechanics. A document should be consistent in how it treats items like verb tense, punctuation, acronyms, professional titles, and numbers. Does the document use *percent* in some places and *per cent* or *%* in others? Is there an opening parenthesis or quotation mark but no closing parenthesis or quotation mark? Is the company called Acme in some places and APC in others?

A good style manual will help with consistency in usage. Some examples of style manuals are listed on the next page.

Formatting. A document should be consistent in format. This means it should have the same general appearance throughout. Many organizations insist on consistent formatting in their letters, memos, and other documents to help identify them to outsiders and distinguish them from others. Formatting is discussed in the next lesson.

In long documents consistency is especially important. In a report, for example, all headings at the same level should be in the same font and size. Pages and footnotes should be numbered in the correct order. Figures should not be labeled *Figure 1*, *Figure 2* and later *Figure C*, *Figure D*.

Word processing programs have many features that help with consistency in formatting. These include search and replace, automatic page numbers, automatic headers and footers, and styles.

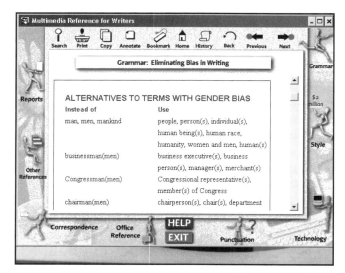

A Style Guide on CD-ROM

Facts. A document should be consistent in terms of facts. For example, suppose the first page of a job posting says the job pays "an hourly rate of $9.75." On page 2, however, the pay is stated as "$7.95 per hour." Obviously, a keying error has been made. Proofreading for consistency means being alert for errors like these and either finding the correct answer yourself or bringing the question to the attention of the writer. Proofreaders should be especially alert for consistency errors in numbers, addresses, and dates.

Aids to Consistency

A useful tool of professional proofreaders is a **style sheet**. A style sheet is a list of items that need to be consistent in a document. An example of a style sheet appears in the Reference Guide folder on your student data disk.

Proofreaders should have a good style manual handy. Some examples are the *Chicago Manual of Style*, the *MLA Handbook for Writers of Research Papers*, and the *Associated Press Stylebook and Libel Manual*. You can find manuals like these at a library. Two good style guides are available online. They are *The Elements of Style* by William Strunk, Jr., at http://www.bartleby.com/141 and the *United States Government Printing Office Style Manual* at http://www.gpoaccess.gov/stylemanual/index.html.

Proofreading for consistency takes concentration, effort, and practice. The results, however, are rewarding. Attention to consistency results in documents that are attractive, easy to read, and easy to understand, all of which conveys an image of your organization—and you—as careful, accurate, detail-oriented, and professional.

Activity 9-1: Proofread Sentences

Proofread the following sentences. Using proofreaders' marks, correct inconsistencies in verb tense, punctuation, and mechanics. If you need help in this or other lesson activities, consult the data disk files *Punctuation* and *Mechanics* in the Reference Guide folder.

1. Please visit us again soon," said Reaves's grandparents.

2. The clerk scheduled two appointments, Monday at 9:45 a.m. and Thursday at ten A.M.

3. Yesterday he keyed the report and had printed two copies.

4. The child enjoyed *Finding Nemo* but was frightened during one scene of "Spider-Man."

5. Before each day's delivery, newspapers must be (1) rolled neatly, 2) banded or placed in a plastic sleeve; and 3. counted.

6. A geyser gets a continuous supply of water that worked its way underground.

7. The 24 chairs cost $320 (twenty were $25.00 each and two were $35 each.

8. Uncle Frank is retired can he crochet!—but he worked for years as a welder.

9. This antivirus software costs sixty-nine fifty as opposed to $39.95 for that software.

10. Jeff is a Community Relations Assistant, and Margaret is an editorial associate.

11. The moon rose in the sky, the night deepened, and suddenly the stars appear.

12. We found that 35 percent of our customers liked the new Web site, 60% found it difficult to use, and five per cent had no opinion.

13. I can e-mail friends in Toronto, Canada; Tokyo, Japan; Sydney; and London, England.

Activity 9-2: **Proofread Paragraphs**

Proofread the two paragraphs below. Using proofreaders' marks, correct inconsistencies in punctuation, mechanics, formatting, and two facts. You will need a dictionary such as *Merriam-Webster Online* (http://www.m-w.com) and a search engine such as Google (http://www.google.com).

Koi are Japanese fish that come in a variety of colors. They measure only one-eighth inch when they hatch. Koi continue to grow until adulthood, reaching eighteen to 24 inches in length, though some have reached a length of nearly five inches. Adult length depends on (a) nutrition, b) water conditions, and (C) genetics. Though koi thrive in water temperatures between 61 and 75 degrees Fahrenheit, they can survive a pond freezing over if it does not freeze solid and an airhole exists. When the temperature drops below fifty degrees Fahrenheit, Koi hibernate and do not require food. Interestingly, they can be trained to eat from your hand.

Koi can live up to 100 years and will remain healthy if genetics are good, the pond is well filtered and clean of debris; and a good hiding place is available when predators—cats, raccoons, and turtles come to visit. Fortunately, red dragonflies are not predators in our water garden as they are in the children's story "Ming Mei's Dance' by Margo Fallis.

Activity 9-3: **Proofread a Memo**

1 Open the data disk file *Equipment Memo* and save it as *Act9-3si*.

2 Proofread the memo for consistency in punctuation, mechanics, and facts. Check any inconsistencies in facts against the equipment supply list in the data disk file *Equipment Study*.

3 Make any needed corrections, and turn in your final corrected copy.

Activity 9-4: Proofread Board Minutes

1 Open the data disk file *Board Minutes* and save it as *Act9-4si*.

2 Proofread the file for consistency in punctuation, mechanics, formatting, and facts. Check the formatting against the data disk file *Style Guide*. Check the facts against the meeting notes below.

3 Make any needed corrections, and turn in your final corrected copy.

8/19/200-

Called to order by Mark Reston, Chairperson. Mins. of July 15 meeting read & approved.

Theresa Patterson welcomed back from 6-wk combined business & vacation trip to South America. Will provide detailed report @ next regular meeting.

Old business: resurfacing parking area @ south end of complex, selling and closing property at 12308 S. Beach Pkwy. ($2,495,000), disposal of surplus office equipment.

Re parking area, question raised re contractors who could complete project in timely manner. Lan Chen moved to "call for in-state bids only, w/a possible bid opening date of Jan. 1 & a construction completion date of Apr. 1." Seconded by Tom DeLong; discussed & approved unanimously. Appointed to head project: Enrico Philippe, Suzanne Flowers, Perry Ables, Brandon Abraham, Agnes Minyard (all in attendance).

Brief discussion re sale of SB property (closing date 9/30). Mark restated desire to donate surplus office equipment: 3 desktop computers, 3 printers, 1 desk, 3 chairs. Based on suggestions since last meeting, 1st offer will be made to local Boys & Girls Club; 2nd if needed to Mayfield Senior Citizens Center. Margo Friarson, PR Director, said she would extend 1st offer immediately.

New business: James Tysdale reported his promotion to VP for Midwest Operations. Will relocate to Nebraska office immediately. Replacement will be announced @ next meeting.

Evelyn Snyder, Director of Telecommunications, granted 3-month leave of absence. Coworkers agreed to absorb her duties as outlined in attached document. Ms. Snyder requested document be used effectively.

No further business, meeting adjourned.

Activity 9-5: **Proofread Merged Letters**

1 Open the data disk file *Speaker Letters* and save it as *Act9-5si*. This file contains six merged letters. The letters were mistakenly merged and printed before the information in them was proofread.

2 Compare the address information in the letters to the address cards below. Correct any errors you find in the letters.

3 Proofread the letters for consistency in punctuation and mechanics and keyboarding errors. Find a factual inconsistency that appears in every letter's standard information.

4 Make any needed corrections, and turn in your final corrected copy.

Dr. Stephen D. Jones 2604 Stoneridge Drive Tallahassee, FL 32303-1907	Mrs. Jennifer Ables 98 Greensboro Avenue Tuscaloosa, AL 35401-1021	Ms. Helen Thompson 435 Pine Lane Athens, TX 75751-3235
Mr. Jacob Donovich 3542 Lincoln Street S. Fargo, ND 58104-7509	Ms. Naomi Littleton 1698 Linwood Lane Lincoln, NE 68505-9497	Dr. Eleanor J. Melton P.O. Box 1059 Chicago, IL 60690-1059

Activity 9-6: **Proofread a Newsletter**

1 Open the data disk file *Bits and Bytes 12 0-* and save it as *Act 9-6si*.

2 Proofread the newsletter for consistency in punctuation, mechanics, and formatting. Find and note one inconsistency in facts.

3 Make any needed corrections, and turn in your final corrected copy.

Format Common Documents

FOCUS

With the advent of the fax machine and e-mail, people are now able to embarrass themselves in writing hundreds of times faster than ever before.

—Marya W. Holcombe

Format Matters

Proper formatting gains a document a favorable first impression and makes it easier to read and understand. A reader can skim through a properly formatted report to see major points, subpoints, and conclusions quickly. A dense report without headings or references may be difficult to read or may predispose the receiver to have an unfavorable view of the contents, your company, and you.

Companies frequently have their own preferred methods for formatting documents and often provide style guides with these preferences. This lesson presents some widely accepted formats that you can use if your organization does not have its own styles.

Business and Personal Letters

Business letters are usually keyed on company letterhead. Personal letters are keyed on plain paper or personal letterhead. Letters on letterhead begin with a **dateline** (the current date). Letters not using a letterhead begin with a return address.

All letters have six standard parts: the **dateline, letter address, salutation, body, complimentary close,** and **writer's name and title**. Letters sometimes use optional parts such as **reference initials** and **enclosure notations**. Proper placement of these letter parts is illustrated in Figure 1 on page 74.

Letters should have a top margin of 2 inches or should start at least two lines below the letterhead. Use the default settings of your word processing software for the other margins. Any subsequent pages use the default settings for all margins and the heading shown in Figure 2. The heading may be keyed as regular copy or set in a header.

Letters can use either open or mixed punctuation. **Mixed punctuation** means a colon follows the salutation and a comma follows the complimentary close. **Open punctuation** means no punctuation follows the salutation or the complimentary close. A comma after the salutation in a business letter is never appropriate.

LETTERHEAD: Sender's name and address

DATELINE: Date letter is mailed

LETTER ADDRESS: Address of person who will receive letter

SALUTATION: Greeting. Includes *Dear*, title (like *Ms.*, *Dr.*, *Mr.*), and last name.

BODY: Letter's message

COMPLIMENTARY CLOSE: Ending such as *Sincerely yours*

WRITER'S NAME AND TITLE: Writer's handwritten name and keyed name and title

REFERENCE INITIALS: Initials of person who keyed letter (used only if writer did not key it)

ENCLOSURE NOTATION: Notice that item(s) are enclosed with letter. Items may be listed.

Plumbing Supplies
Industrial Products

**KIPMER
SUPPLY COMPANY**

Phone: (618) 555-0151
Fax: (618) 555-0156

P.O. Box 768
100 N. Main • Centralia, IL 62801-6133

October 5, 200– ↓ **4**

> Set date about 2" from top of page
> or at least 2 lines below letterhead.

Mr. Jeb Akin
Jeb's Hardware
204 S. Main
Centralia, IL 62801-6137 ↓ **2**

Dear Mr. Akin ↓ **2**

Thank you for your past business at Kipmer Supply. We appreciate the opportunity to serve you and look forward to working with you in the future.

Satisfied customers are our best advertisement. Enclosed with this letter is a survey we hope will help us serve you even better. As a token of our appreciation for your feedback, your name will be entered in a drawing for $100 worth of merchandise from Kipmer just for filling out the survey. Bring in the survey/raffle ticket and drop it in our sink at 100 N. Main in Centralia.

We also want to take this opportunity to introduce you to our new staff via the enclosed newsletter. In the meantime, if you have any questions or require assistance, please feel free to contact me. ↓ **2**

Sincerely ↓ **4**

Roger Kipmer, President
Kipmer Supply ↓ **2**

bn ↓ **2**

Enclosures

default

default ... *default*

Figure 1: Business Letter in Block Format

Use default margins and plain paper.

Mr. Vincent Petrosino
Page 2
February 2, 200- ↓ **2**

We are delighted you will be joining us on Tuesday for the annual meeting. Would you please bring the copy of the agenda I sent you last week?

Figure 2: Heading for Subsequent Pages

---

102 W. Hanover St.
New Baden, IL 62265-1715
September 1, 200- ↓ **4**

Mrs. Imogene Harris
Business Chairperson
Chidrow High School
6420 Main St.
Bonners Ferry, ID 83805-8520

Figure 3: Setup for a Letter not on Letterhead

Interoffice Memorandums

Messages sent to persons within an organization are called **memorandums** or **memos**. Memos are a quick way to communicate with one or many employees. Memos can be prepared using preprinted forms, templates or wizards from word processing programs, or plain paper. Figure 4 shows the proper way to format a memo.

Job titles and department names for the sender and receiver are optional. Titles such as *Mr.* and *Dr.* are occasionally used for the receiver. Courtesy titles are not generally used for the sender. Memos may have some of the same optional parts as letters, such as reference initials or an enclosure notation, and these parts are placed in the same way. Second and subsequent pages of memos are formatted as in Figure 2.

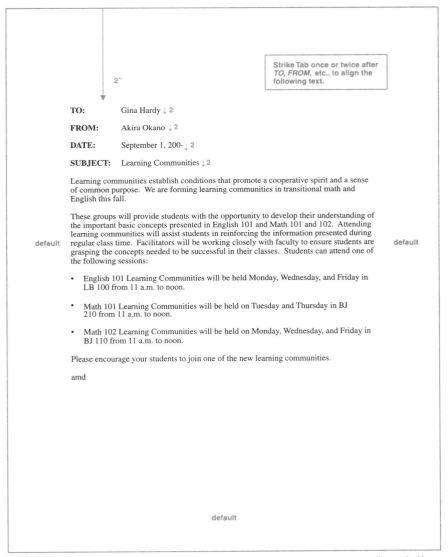

HEADINGS: Receiver's name, sender's name, date memo is sent, and memo's subject

BODY: Memo's message

REFERENCE INITIALS: Initials of person who keyed memo (used only if writer did not key it)

Figure 4: **Memo**

Reports

Reports provide and analyze information. Examples of business reports include minutes of meetings, speeches, financial reports, journal articles, and proposals. Examples of school reports include themes, book reports, and term papers. The parts included in a report vary depending upon the type of report, length, and degree of formality.

Figures 5 and 6 are examples of pages from an unbound educational report. An **unbound report** is a report without a binder: The pages are held together by a paper clip or staple. Generally, educational reports are double spaced, and business reports are single spaced. The other formatting is the same, except that single-spaced reports have double spacing between paragraphs, and the paragraphs begin at the left margin.

When proofreading a report, check for correct formatting and consistency among report parts. For example, check that side headings always have initial capital letters and are always bold. Check reference information for accuracy.

TITLE: 14-point, bold, all capital letters, centered

BODY: 12-point, double-spaced, 0.5-inch first-line indent for paragraphs

SIDE HEADINGS: Bold with initial capital letters for first word and important words. Begin at left margin.

PAGE BREAKS: Keep headings with their following paragraphs. If breaking a paragraph, leave at least two lines on the first page and carry at least two lines to the next page.

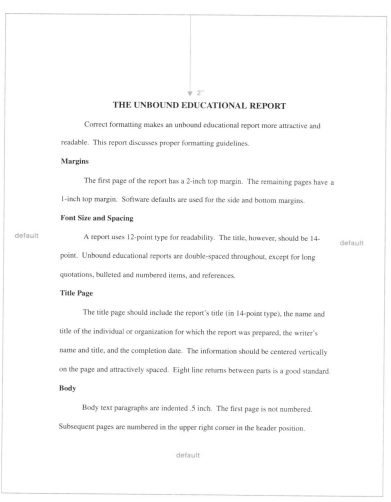

Figure 5: **Page 1 of an Unbound Educational Report**

Proofreading Tips

> When proofreading a long report, proofread all similar parts as a separate step. Check the format of all side headings; then check all paragraph headings. Check that all numbered pages, tables, and figures are in order.

> When preparing a report or other long document, create a style sheet showing how unusual features, such as names, titles, or special terms, will be handled.

1"   2

Main heading. The main heading is centered horizontally. It is in capital letters, 14-point type, and bold.

Side headings. Side headings begin at the left margin. They are bold, and the first letter of the first word and of each important word is capitalized.

Paragraph headings. Paragraph headings begin at paragraph point and are bold. Only the first letter of the first word is capitalized, along with the first letter of any word that would ordinarily be capitalized. Paragraph headings end with a period.

References heading. A references heading is centered, in capital letters, in 14-point, and bold. The heading may read *REFERENCES* or *BIBLIOGRAPHY*.

References

default   A popular method of documenting sources in a report is internal citations. An   default

internal citation consists of the last name(s) of the author(s), the publication date, and the page number(s). It appears in parentheses in the body of the report, after the cited material (VanHuss, Forde, and Woo, 2002, 130).

References appear in alphabetical order on the last page of the report if they will all fit. If not, they appear on a separate page with a 2-inch top margin. References are single-spaced, with double spacing between them, and are set in hanging indent format.

REFERENCE

VanHuss, Susie H., Forde, Connie M., and Woo, Donna L. *College Keyboarding and Word Processing, Microsoft® Word 2002.* Cincinnati: South-Western, 2002.

default

PAGE NUMBERS: Upper right corner of all pages except first page. Use word processor page numbering feature.

PARAGRAPH HEADINGS: Bold with initial capital letter for first word and words that are always capitalized. Begin at paragraph point; end with period.

REFERENCES: On last page if all will fit; if not, on separate page with 2-inch top margin. Single-spaced with double spacing between; 0.5-inch hanging indent.

Figure 6: **Page 2 of an Unbound Educational Report**

Electronic Mail

Electronic mail or **e-mail** is a popular alternative to memos and sometimes to business letters. Electronic mail is a means of sending messages from one computer to another. It is a quick, inexpensive way to communicate with one or many people.

Electronic mail is set up like a memo. The recipient's e-mail address is keyed in the *To* field or selected from a list. A brief subject line is keyed in the *Subject* field. The program fills in the sender's e-mail address and the date and time the message was sent. Paragraphs are single spaced, with a blank line between them. Some writers begin with a brief salutation, such as *Hi Thomas* or *Mr. Smith*, and then press Enter twice to key the body of the e-mail. Writers may include their names, two lines below the last paragraph.

E-mail does not require any formatting. Except for simple formatting such as bold, formatting should be avoided because the recipient's e-mail software may not support it.

Facsimiles or Faxes

A **facsimile** or **fax** is a document sent electronically from one machine to another. Faxing is a rapid and convenient way to send hard-copy information. A fax should always be accompanied by a cover sheet (Figure 7). Short messages may be keyed directly on the cover sheet to save paper and transmission time.

A fax cover sheet must include all the following information:

> The date of the fax
> The receiver's full name
> The receiver's fax number
> The receiver's phone number

> The sender's full name
> The sender's fax number
> The sender's phone number
> The number of pages being sent

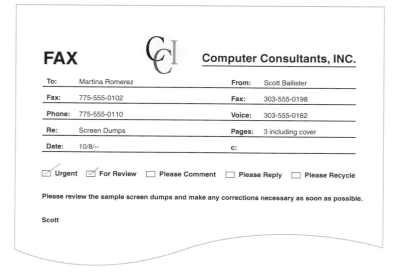

Fax machines are commonly shared by many persons within a company. Confidential information should not be faxed except in an emergency.

Figure 7: **Fax Cover Sheet**

Activity 10-1: Check Letter and Memo Parts

In each pair of letter or memo parts shown below, one example is correctly formatted and the other is incorrectly formatted. Put a check mark in the box next to the correctly formatted example. Apply proofreaders' marks to any errors you find in the incorrect example.

For the activities in this lesson, refer to the model documents on pages 74–78 and the *Format* file in the Reference Guide on your student data disk for examples of correct formatting.

☐   Mr. George Oza
1002 S. Market Street
Wilmington, DE 19801-5228

☐   George Oza
1002 S. Market Street
Wilmington, Del. 19801-5228

☐   Jan. 4, 200-

Sara Wilfong
900 Abbott Rd.
East Lansing Michigan

☐   January 4, 200-

Ms. Sara Wilfong
900 Abbott Rd.
East Lansing, MI 48823-3105

☐   Sincerely Yours,

James H. Turner

☐   Sincerely yours,

James H. Turner

James H. Turner

☐   Adam Estevez

kd

Enclosure

☐   Adam Estevez

enclosure

KD

☐   Date: 4 March 200-

To: Sam Tillery

From: Eva St. John

Subject: sales conference

☐   **TO:**   Sam Tillery

FROM: Eva St. John

DATE: March 4, 200-

SUBJECT: Sales Conference

Activity 10-2: Proofread a Business Letter for Formatting Errors

Proofread the following letter for formatting and keyboarding errors. Apply proofreaders' marks to any errors you find in the letter.

 CHAMBERS UNIVERSITY

3501 Wynola Road * Julian, CA 92036-9630 * (760) 555-0136 * http://www.chambers.edu

July 15, 200-

Mr. Jonathan McGreggor
1878 Apple Street
Portage, Mich. 49002-5736

Dear Mr. McGreggor,

On behalf of the housing department of Chambers University, congradulations on your admission to this year's freshman class.

Your stay in a residence hall will be   one of the most rewarding and memorable aspects of your university career. Living in a residence hall places you at the heart of campus life. You will be able to walk to and from classes, dining facilities, the library, athletic facilities, and health services. You will have the the opportunity to make lifelong friendships with a variety of individuals from many places. Our residence hall staff offers a wide range of services and programs that foster personal growth and involvement both inside an outside the academic community.

The Chambers University housing department houses more than 3,000 undergraduate and graduate students in ten unique residence halls. The housing office, located in Carpathia Hall, handles they application and assignment process for residences. Please fill out the enclosed application form and return it to us by **August 1.** If you have questions, you may e-mail us at housing@chambers.edu or call us at (618) 555-0138 from 8 a.m. to 4 p.m. Monday through Friday.

Once again, welcome to Chambers University. We wish you great success in your univresity career.

Sincerely Yours,

JoAnn Glibonski
Director of Housing

bn

Activity 10-3: Proofread a Personal Letter for Formatting Errors

1　Open the data disk file *James Fiore* and save it as *Act 10-3si*.

2　Proofread the letter for formatting errors. Use the United States Postal Service Web site at http://www.usps.com to find the correct ZIP Code for the return address. Obtain the ZIP Code for the letter address from Activity 10-2.

3　Make any needed corrections, and turn in your final corrected copy.

Activity 10-4: Create a Memo Template and Memo

1　Create a new document with the following header in 16-point Arial bold and a rule beneath it:

Office of the Principal　　　　　Memorandum

2　Key the header lines for a memo (*To, From, Date, and Subject*).

3　Save your document as a **template** called *Act 10-4Asi* (in Microsoft® Word, Save As/Document Template).

4　Using your new memo template, key the text below as a memorandum. Compose an appropriate subject line, and key your initials as the reference initials.

5　Save your document as a **document** called *Act 10-4Bsi* (in Microsoft® Word, Save As/Word Document) and proofread it.

From Fred Perkins, Principal

To Jan Parkinson, Student Affairs, July 10, 200-

On a recent visit to Mt. Airy Community College, I learned about a mentoring program in place for incoming freshmen. According to the admissions director, students have overwhelmingly expressed their satisfaction with the program.

I am considering whether we should institute such a program at our school. Let's get together to discuss this idea sometime in the next two weeks. The enclosed brochure will give you information about the Mt. Airy program.

When you are ready to meet, please have Beverly schedule a half-hour appointment. I look forward to hearing your thoughts on this topic.

Activity 10-5: Proofread and Format a Two-Page Letter

1 Open the data disk file *Junior Night Letter* and save it as *Act10-5si*.

2 Proofread the letter for formatting and keyboarding errors.

3 Make any needed corrections, and turn in your final corrected copy.

Activity 10-6: Compose a Personal Letter

1 Compose a personal letter to Mr. John H. Skibinski, Director of the Office of Admissions and Scholarships at Chambers University, at the address given in the Activity 10-2 letter. Explain that you are considering applying to Chambers University, and request the following:

> Information on classes and test scores required for admission

> Information on scholarships based on high school academics, activities, and ACT or SAT scores

> A current catalog

> An application for admission

2 Use today's date for your letter. Save it as *Act10-6si* and proofread it.

Activity 10-7: Create a Fax Cover Sheet

Ms. Janice Grabowski did not receive the letter about Junior Night that you proofread in Activity 10-5 as did her classmates. She has asked the Office of the Principal to fax a copy of her letter to her at 513-555-0127, which is both her home telephone number and her fax number.

Create a fax cover sheet for the letter. Use a word processor template or design the cover sheet yourself. The fax number for Cincinnati West High School is 513-555-0146. Use today's date. Save your document as *Act10-7si* and proofread it.

Activity 10-8: Format and Proofread a Report

1 Form a team with two other students. Open the data disk file *Aid Report* and save it as *Act10-8si*.

2 Format the document as an unbound report and proofread it for formatting and keyboarding errors. Single-space bulleted items, and use double spacing between them.

3 Make any needed corrections, and turn in your final corrected copy.

Simulation

Around-the-World Travel Club

You are interested in a career in the travel industry. Recently, you have been looking for an internship or part-time job to help you decide whether this career path is right for you. You have been contacting travel agencies, checking the help-wanted ads in the newspaper, and visiting your school placement office. In today's paper, you found the following advertisement.

Job 1: Create a Resume and Application Letter

Prepare a resume and letter of application for the student intern position. Make sure your resume and letter are error-free. Use the current date for the letter. Save your work as *Job1Asi* and *Job1Bsi*.

Around-the-World Travel Club

Student Intern

Around-the-World Travel Club has an immediate opening for a student intern. The student intern will report directly to the Executive Director of Around-the-World Travel Club, a private organization with 25,000 members worldwide.

The successful candidate will have superior problem-solving and communications skills. Excellent Microsoft® Word, Microsoft® Excel, and Microsoft® Access skills are essential, as well as skills in the Microsoft® PowerPoint® presentation graphics program. The position will be responsible for a variety of duties, including communications with members and suppliers. Job tasks include composing, editing, and proofreading communications as well as keeping a detailed database. The candidate should also be able to do effective research on the Internet.

This job will be 20 hours a week for 36 weeks. It is a great opportunity for someone wanting to enter the travel industry. Please send a resume and letter of application to:

Jill Brown, Executive Director
Around-the-World Travel Club
2710 W. Clay
St. Charles, MO 63301-2553
Phone: 636-555-0120
Fax: 636-555-0121

Around-the-World Travel is an equal opportunity employer.

Job 2: Complete a Job Application

Jill Brown, executive director of Around-the-World Travel Club, has invited you for an interview. Fill out the following job application neatly and completely. Use today's date. Make sure your work is accurate.

Application for Employment

1. Position applied for		2. Social Security No.	

3. Name				4. Home	
	Last	First	Middle		Phone

5. Address				6. Work	
	Street	City	State	ZIP Code	Phone

7. EDUCATION

a. Check highest grade completed. ❑1 ❑2 ❑3 ❑4 ❑5 ❑6 ❑7 ❑8 ❑9 ❑10 ❑11 ❑12 | Year |

b. If you did not complete high school, do you have a high school equivalency diploma? ❑ Yes ❑ No | Date |

c. Check number of years of post-high school education. ❑1 ❑2 ❑3 ❑4 ❑5 ❑6 ❑7

Name and Location of Institution	Hours	Degree	Major or Specialty	Dates Attended

8. EXPERIENCE—Starting with the most recent, describe *ALL* paid and applicable volunteer experience. Highlight knowledge, skills, and abilities that best demonstrate your qualifications for this position. May we contact your present supervisor? ❑ Yes ❑ No

a. **Job Title**		Duties			
Employer					
Address				Phone	
Supervisor		Title		Hrs./week	
Salary (start)		(finish)	Equipment used		
Dates	to (mo/yr)		Reason for leaving		

b. **Job Title**		Duties			
Employer					
Address				Phone	
Supervisor		Title		Hrs./week	
Salary (start)		(finish)	Equipment used		
Dates	to (mo/yr)		Reason for leaving		

c. Use this space for any additional information you think would help us evaluate your application, including training, seminars, workshops, and special achievements or specialized skills.

d. Licenses (to include driver), certificates, or other authorizations to practice a trade or profession

9. REFERENCES—List names, addresses, and relationships of two persons not related to you who know your qualifications.

Name	Address	Phone	Relationship

Have you ever been convicted of any violation(s) of law, including moving traffic violations? ❑ Yes ❑ No

If yes, provide a description of the offense, the place, and the dates of charges and convictions on a separate piece of paper.

10. When will you be available to start work (month, day, year)?

11. **CERTIFICATION**—I certify that all entries on this form are true and complete. I consent to references, former employers, and educational institutions listed being contacted regarding this application.

Date		Signature	

Job 3: **Proofread a Flyer**

Congratulations on your new position as student intern at Around-the-World Travel Club! You will report to Jill Brown, executive director. Ms. Brown has asked you to proofread and correct a flyer about a December holiday skiing trip that the events planner has organized. The file named *Breckenridge* is the Travel Club folder on your data disk. Save your work as *Job3si*.

Job 4: **Proofread Tips for Travelers**

Around-the-World Travel Club is putting together a manual with tips for travelers. Ms. Brown wrote the section on water use in foreign countries that appears below. She has asked you to compare this document with the copy her secretary keyed and correct any errors. The keyed copy is in the data disk file *Manual Water*. Save your work as *Job4si*.

Water

The availability of fresh, pure water is sometimes a concern for world travelers. When you are traveling to a foreign county with questionable water sources, Around-the-World recommends that you consume only:

→ Bevrages made with boiled water.
→ Canned or bottled carbonated beverages, such as carbonated bottled water.

You should also take the following precautions:

→ Do not drink beverages with ice.
→ drink beverages from cans or bottles rather than glasses.
→ Dry off wet cans before opening.
→ Wipe off the part of the can that will be in contact with your mouth.
→ Do not brush your teeth with tap water.

Job 5: **Research Passport Information**

Ms. Brown has asked you to research how to obtain a U.S. passport. Your findings will be included in the manual for travelers that you worked on in Job 4. Do your research on the Internet, and respond to Ms. Brown with a memo. Find out how to obtain a passport, what form(s) are needed, and how to keep your passport safe while traveling. Include any other information you think would be useful for travelers. Use today's date. Provide the Web addresses you used for your research. Save your memo as *Job5si*.

Job 6: Proofread Web Pages

Around-the-World Travel Club is updating its Web site. Ms. Brown has asked you to proofread some of the new material that will appear on the site. Proofread the data disk files *Opening Page Around-the-World Travel Club* and *Mountain Air and Mountain Music*. Check facts carefully and correct any errors. Save the files **with the same filenames** so the links will work.

Job 7: Proofread and Compose Autobiographical Sketches

The new opening page for the Around-the-World Web site will include a brief autobiography of its newest staff member—you! Ms. Brown has asked you to proofread her autobiography and use it as a guide in composing your own. Because of limited Web page space, your sketch is limited to 50 words or less.

Save your autobiography as *Job7si* and copy it to the *Opening Page Around-the-World Travel Club* document you corrected in Job 6. Remember to **save this document with the same filename** so the links will work.

> As a child, i dreamed of been a world traveler; visiting famous citys, and meeting intresting people. After earning my b.a. in history from Chambers u., , I moved to Atlanta, found employment with a travel agency, and tried my best to learn everything about the bussiness. I traveled to ninety-five countries, led dozens of tour groups, and arrange travel for thousands of clients.
>
> When my agency started the Around-the-World Travel Club. I was offered the opportunity to move to Saint   Charles with a promotion to Exec. Dir. Researching and planning vacations for clients, as well as having the opportunity to travel around the world my self, gifts me much satisfaction.

Job 8: Do Travel Research on the Internet

Around-the-World plans to offer trips to the Florida Keys. Mr. Duper has asked you to conduct some research on the Keys. Open the data disk file *Florida Keys Scavenger Hunt* and save it as *Job8si*. Use the hyperlink in this document for the Florida Keys to conduct your research.

Job 9: **Proofread a Promotional Guide**

A promotional guide for a Florida Keys vacation will be mailed to clients. Mr. Duper designed this guide from your scavenger hunt research. He has asked you to proofread it. Check facts by referring to the material you gathered in Job 8. You may also visit the Best of the Florida Keys Web site at http://thefloridakeys.com/about_the_keys.htm.

Around-the-World Travel

presents:

THE FLORIDA KEYS— ADVENTURE OF A LIFE TIME!

APRIL 11–17, 200-

Travel with us on a luxury bus for a week of adventure. It begins with a tour of **Everglade National Park,** the largest US park East of the Rocky Mountains. We'll walk though spectacular wet lands with a ranger as our guide and enjoy hiking, canoeing, or fishing—no license required!

Then its on to **the Keys,** 160 miles of ilands that offer something for every travelers' tastes. Are first stop is **Key Largo,** where we'll take a glass-bottomed boat tour at **Loue Key National Marine Sanctuary.** You can shop,relax on the beach, and maybe try parasaling!

We'll travel to **Islamorada,** the "island of bones" and sport fishing capital of the world. Enjoy water sports, entertainment, and a sumptuous dinner at a restaurant on the bay!

Our next stop is **Log Key,** to enjoy a quite day in one of the Key's most secluded locations. Then it's on to **Marathon** for fun on the water, at the beach, or in its' shops and museum!

At **Big Pine Key,** we'll visit **Louie Key National Marine Sanctuary,** home of what's been called the most spectacular reef in the lower keys. You'll enjoy the reef your way—skin diving, snorlkeing, fishing, or boating!

Our last stop is fabulous **Key West.** You'll follow in Ernest Hemingway's foot steps as you walk down **Duvall Street,** with stops at the many eateries and art galleries along the way. Then we'll come together to watch the sun go down at **Sunset Fest.** With exciting music and carnival acts it will be a fantastic ending to your Florida Key adventure.

For farther information, contact:

Erik Duper, Event Planner

erik@aroundtheworldtravel.com

800-555-0122

Job 10: **Proofread Letters to Clients**

Around-the-World Travel Club maintains a database of clients who have booked trips in the past. It also includes people who have signed up for the club's mailing list. Ms. Brown has asked you to proofread letters to clients who asked to be notified about Florida Keys vacations.

Open the address information disk file *Keys Promo Letters*. Compare the data in the letters to the database printout below. Check facts by referring to the material you gathered in Job 8 or by visiting the Best of the Florida Keys Web site at http://thefloridakeys.com/about_the_keys.htm. Save the file as *Job10si*.

LAST	FIRST	TI	STREET	CITY	ST	ZIP+4	DESTINATION	DATE	NIGHTS	#ADLTS	#CHILD
Jackson	Timothy	Mr.	3601 Carriage Lane	Douglasville	GA	30135-3421	CO - Breckenridge	12/20/200-	9	2	3
Thurston	Frank	Mr.	91 Christine Court	Rockport	ME	04856-4811	CO - Breckenridge	12/20/200-	6	2	0
Michael	Donald	Mr.	2201 Arrowhead Drive	Carson City	NV	89706-0459	CO - Breckenridge	12/20/200-	6	1	0
Whitfield	Daniel	Mr.	321 Adam Street	Richland	MS	39218-9518	CO - Breckenridge	12/20/200-	6	2	1
Smith	Dave	Mr.	21903 Cherry Hill Street	Dearborn	MI	48128-1148	FL - Florida Keys	06/19/200-	6	2	0
Vines	Vance	Mr.	204 Angus Drive	Luling	LA	70070-4427	FL - Florida Keys	06/05/200-	6	2	0
Kohler	Wayne	Mr.	601 Sable Drive	Centralia	IL	62801-4472	FL - Florida Keys	10/02/200-	6	2	2
Panky	Mary	Ms.	197 Water Street	Grenada	MS	38901-2427	FL - Florida Keys	06/05/200-	6	1	1
James	Philip	Mr.	PO Box 2394	Port Arthur	TX	77643-2394	FL - Florida Keys	10/02/200-	6	2	0
Jimmerson	Otto	Mr.	3151 Windland Drive	Green Bay	WI	54311-7607	TN - Gaitlinburg	09/04/200-	6	2	0
Pinkston	Samuel	Mr.	495 Dakota Avenue	Columbus	OH	43223-1531	TN - Gaitlinburg	09/11/200-	13	2	0
McDaniel	Evelyn	Mrs.	29206 Prairie Place	Pierre	SD	57501-6318	TN - Gaitlinburg	09/11/200-	6	2	0
Myers	Charlie	Mr.	1001 Oak Avenue	Panama City	FL	32401-2463	TN - Gaitlinburg	06/05/200-	6	2	2
Herrington	Janet	Mrs.	1140 Jeffery Drive	Birmingham	AL	35235-2661	TN - Gaitlinburg	05/29/200-	3	2	0
Oslo	Janine	Ms.	139 Abbott Road	Fremont	NH	03044-3401	TN - Gaitlinburg	09/25/200-	6	1	0

Record: 16 of 16

GREYSCALE

BIN TRAVELER FORM

Cut By _____Ana Torrado_____ Qty__60__ Date_04/23/25_

Scanned By_____ Qty_____Date_____

Scanned Batch IDs

_____   _____   _____

Notes / Exception

_____

_____

_____

_____

_____